Related Services
in Special Education

SPECIAL EDUCATION LAW, POLICY, AND PRACTICE

Series Editors
Mitchell L. Yell, PhD, University of South Carolina
David F. Bateman, PhD, American Institutes for Research

The *Special Education Law, Policy, and Practice* series highlights current trends and legal issues in the education of students with disabilities. The books in this series link legal requirements with evidence-based instruction and highlight practical applications for working with students with disabilities. The titles in the *Special Education Law, Policy, and Practices* series are designed not only to be required textbooks for general education and special education preservice teacher education programs but are also designed for practicing teachers, education administrators, principals, school counselors, school psychologists, parents, and others interested in improving the lives of students with disabilities. The *Special Education Law, Policy, and Practice* series is committed to research-based practices working to provide appropriate and meaningful educational programming for students with disabilities and their families.

Titles in Series:

The Essentials of Special Education Law by Andrew M. Markelz and David F. Bateman

Special Education Law Annual Review 2020 by David F. Bateman, Mitchell L. Yell, and Kevin P. Brady

Developing Educationally Meaningful and Legally Sound IEPs by Mitchell L. Yell, David F. Bateman, and James G. Shriner

Sexuality Education for Students with Disabilities edited by Thomas C. Gibbon, Elizabeth A. Harkins Monaco, and David F. Bateman

Creating Positive Elementary Classrooms: Preventing Behavior Challenges to Promote Learning by Stephen W. Smith and Mitchell L. Yell

Service Animals in Schools: Legal, Educational, Administrative, and Strategic Handling Aspects by Anne O. Papalia, Kathy B. Ewoldt, and David F. Bateman

Evidence-Based Practices for Supporting Individuals with Autism Spectrum Disorder edited by Laura C. Chezan, Katie Wolfe, and Erik Drasgow

Special Education Law Annual Review 2021 by David F. Bateman, Mitchell L. Yell, and Kevin P. Brady

Dispute Resolution under the IDEA: Understanding, Avoiding, and Managing Special Education Disputes by David F. Bateman, Mitchell L. Yell, and Jonas Dorego

Advocating for the Common Good: People, Politics, Process, and Policy on Capitol Hill by Jane E. West

Related Services in Special Education: Working Together as a Team by Lisa Goran and David F. Bateman

Related Services in Special Education

Working Together as a Team

Lisa Goran, PhD, CCC-SLP
University of Missouri

David F. Bateman, PhD
American Institutes for Research

ROWMAN & LITTLEFIELD
Lanham • Boulder • New York • London

Published by Rowman & Littlefield
An imprint of The Rowman & Littlefield Publishing Group, Inc.
4501 Forbes Boulevard, Suite 200, Lanham, Maryland 20706
www.rowman.com

86-90 Paul Street, London EC2A 4NE

Copyright © 2024 by The Rowman & Littlefield Publishing Group, Inc.

All rights reserved. No part of this book may be reproduced in any form or by any electronic or mechanical means, including information storage and retrieval systems, without written permission from the publisher, except by a reviewer who may quote passages in a review.

British Library Cataloguing in Publication Information Available

Library of Congress Cataloging-in-Publication Data

Names: Goran, Lisa, author. | Bateman, David, 1963- author.
Title: Related services in special education : working together as a team / Lisa Goran, David F. Bateman.
Description: Lanham, Maryland : Rowman & Littlefield, 2024. | Series: Special education law, policy, and practice | Includes bibliographical references and index. | Summary: "A resource for all members of an IEP team to work together more intentionally and effectively to support students, this book showcases the professional expertise and the value related services providers bring to the IEP team and school community and offers multiple resources to support on-going learning and connection"— Provided by publisher.
Identifiers: LCCN 2023006932 (print) | LCCN 2023006933 (ebook) | ISBN 9781538168820 (cloth) | ISBN 9781538168837 (paperback) | ISBN 9781538168844 (epub)
Subjects: LCSH: School-linked human services—United States. | Special education—United States. | Individualized education programs—United States. | Special education teachers—Professional relationships—United States. | Special education—Law and legislation—United States.
Classification: LCC LB3013.55 .G67 2024 (print) | LCC LB3013.55 (ebook) | DDC 371.90973—dc23/eng/20230313
LC record available at https://lccn.loc.gov/2023006932
LC ebook record available at https://lccn.loc.gov/2023006933

With gratitude to Brittni (Campbell) Johnson

Brief Contents

Acknowledgments	xv
Introduction	xvii
1 Related Services	1
2 Requirements and Considerations of Related Services	21
3 Types and Examples of Related Services	41
4 Transportation as a Related Service	53
5 Health Care Supports as a Related Service	81
6 Roles of Related-Service Providers	97
7 Recommended Resources	115
Appendix A: Case Studies	129
Case Study 1: Max	129
Case Study 2: Saraiah	131
Case Study 3: Angelus	132
Appendix B: Supreme Court Cases Involving Related Services	135
Irving Independent School District v. Tatro (1984)	135
Cedar Rapids Community School District v. Garret F. (1999)	139
Key Terms	141
References	145
Index	147
About the Authors	153

Contents

Acknowledgments   xv

Introduction   xvii

1   Related Services   1
    Definition and Purpose of Related Services   1
    Related Services and the IEP   2
    Related Services   3
        How?   4
        What?   4
            Not Exhaustive yet Alphabetical List of Related Services   4
        When?   5
        Evaluation and Progress Monitoring   6
        Cost   7
        Exclusions   7
    Specific Related Services   9
        Art Therapy   9
        Assistive Technology   10
        Audiology Services   10
        Counseling Services   11
        Early Identification and Assessment of Disabilities in Children   11
        Interpreting Services   12
        Occupational Therapy   12
        Orientation and Mobility Services   12
        Parent/Guardian Counseling and Training   13
        Physical Therapy   13
        Psychological Services   13
        Recreation   14

Rehabilitation Counseling	14
School Health and School Nurse Services	15
Social Work Services in Schools	15
Speech-Language Pathology	16
Transportation	16
Important and Connected Points	17
Summary and Key Points	17
Active Learning Engagement	18
Key Terms	18
Questions to Consider	19
2 Requirements and Considerations of Related Services	**21**
Specifics Related to the IEP	21
12 IEP Tips	22
Tip 1	22
Tip 2	22
Tip 3	23
Tip 4	23
Tip 5	23
Tip 6	23
Tip 7	23
Tip 8	24
Tip 9	24
Tip 10	24
Tip 11	24
Tip 12	24
Clarity on the Services Provided	25
IEP Purposes	25
Communication	25
Annual Performance Goals	25
Services Provided	25
Evaluation	26
Management	26
Accountability	26
Compliance and Monitoring	27
Contract	27
Required IEP Components	27
Demographics	28
IEP Team Signatures	28
Notice of Procedural Safeguards	28
Special Considerations	28

Present Levels of Academic Achievement and Functional Performance (PLAAFP)	29
Goals and Objectives	29
Supports for the General Education Teacher in the IEP	30
Extended School Year (ESY)	31
Placement	31
Least Restrictive Environment	32
Reevaluation	32
IEP Team Member with Typical Roles	33
Summary of a Typical IEP Meeting	35
Four Important IEP Points for Classroom Teachers	36
Summary	38
Key Terms	38
Questions to Consider	39

3 Types and Examples of Related Services — 41

Communication Services	42
Speech-Language	42
Audiological Services	43
Interpreting Services	43
Physical Services	44
Orientation and Mobility	44
Physical Therapy	44
Occupational Therapy	44
Recreational Therapy	45
Social, Emotional, and Psychological Services	45
Psychological Services	45
Social Work Services in Schools	46
Parent Counseling and Training	47
Medical and Health Services	47
School Health Services and School Nurse Services	48
Medical Services for Diagnostic or Evaluation Purposes	48
Miscellaneous Special Services	49
Early Identification and Assessment of Disabilities in Children	49
Transportation	49
Summary	49
Key Terms	50
Questions to Consider	51
Individual	51
Schoolwide Community	51
IEP Paperwork, Team, and Process	51

4	**Transportation as a Related Service**	53
	Summary	71
	Key Terms	71
	Questions to Consider	72
5	**Health Care Supports as a Related Service**	81
	Summary	91
	Key Terms	91
	Questions to Consider	92
6	**Roles of Related-Service Providers**	97
	Related-Service Providers as, Well, Service Providers	98
	Related-Service Providers as Collaborators	100
	Related-Service Providers as Professional Experts	101
	Related-Service Providers as Communicators	102
	Within the Team	103
	With Parents	103
	With External Service Providers	103
	With Administrators	104
	Related-Service Providers as IEP Team Members	105
	IEP Paperwork	105
	IEP Meeting	105
	Tips for Effective Communication	106
	A Day in the Life of a Related-Service Provider	107
	A Day in the Life: Baleigh	108
	A Day in the Life: Mallory	111
	Summary	113
	Key Terms	114
	Questions to Consider	114
7	**Recommended Resources**	115
	Books	116
	National Organizations and Resources for	
	Related-Service Providers	117
	Communication Services	117
	Physical Services	117
	Social, Emotional, and Psychological Services	117
	Medical and Health Services	117
	Online Resources	118
	The Regulations for Related Services	118
	Words of Advice	123
	Related-Service Words of Advice	123
	Key Terms	127
	Questions to Consider	127

Appendix A: Case Studies — 129
    Case Study 1: Max — 129
    Case Study 2: Saraiah — 131
    Case Study 3: Angelus — 132

Appendix B: Supreme Court Cases Involving Related Services — 135
    Irving Independent School District v. Tatro (1984) — 135
    Cedar Rapids Community School District v. Garret F. (1999) — 139

Key Terms — 141

References — 145

Index — 147

About the Authors — 153

Acknowledgments

We wish to thank the below reviewers whose thoughtful comments and expertise guided our writing and revisions for the development of this book. As always, any errors and omissions are our own:

Pam Epler, *Grand Canyon University*
Roberta Gentry, *University of Virginia*
Elizabeth Harkins, *William Paterson University*
Stacey Heiligenthaler, PhD, *Greenwich Public Schools*
Sherie Huber, *Illinois Council for Exceptional Children; Glen Ellyn Public School District #41 (retired)*
Gloria Niles, *University of Hawaiʻi*
Gayle Willey, *Missouri Council of Administrators of Special Education*

Introduction

Thank you. Just by opening this book and reading this first sentence, you are engaging with us in a very important conversation. Related services are an essential component of many individualized education programs (IEPs) for students who need special education services, but too many of us in education don't know what they are; who provides them; or how those professionals can be active, valuable members of the team and school community. We hope this book helps change that.

Please note: We do not assign blame here. We recognize every role in education—from elementary teacher to school counselor to 8th-grade math teacher to vice principal to special educator—requires specialized training and knowledge learned through educator-preparation programs, practice, and real-world experience. Special education truly is individualized, and every student presents with a different array of needs. There is no way your preparation program could have taught you everything you need to know to work with every single student who is educated in your school. There is no way for you to know what you don't know as you embark on a new school year and work with new colleagues, new students, and new family dynamics. We hope this book fills in some gaps about related services and related-service professionals, as well as leads you to ask even more questions, access additional resources, and engage in new ways with both these ideas and your school teams.

We wrote this book with you in mind. We want to provide you information about related services, along with ways to connect this information to everyday practice. With this goal of combining information and connection, we include three case studies of students who receive special education services and require related services. We intentionally created these case studies with varying levels of need and complexity. They progress from fairly simple to more complex. No sample student is a direct representation of any one student we've known; we developed these case studies from an amalgamation of situations we've experienced, students we've known, and services we wish had been provided over decades of work in special education. David drew from his experiences as a special educator, hearing officer, teacher educator, and advocate. Lisa drew from her experiences as a speech-language pathologist, special educator, teacher educator, advocate, and person with disabilities. We both drew from stories shared by teachers we've connected with across the nation and supported over the years.

We also wrote this book as a resource for you, something you can turn to time and again. This is not intended to be a book you read through once and then leave to collect dust on a shelf. With ongoing value in mind, we've included multiple resources you can explore and use in your own practice, resources we hope you'll return to again and again as you support students with disabilities and work with the professionals who provide the services they need.

As you continue this conversation with us, we hope the book's structure is helpful to you. The first two chapters are the general information and requirements for related services. Chapter 3 includes a little more information about the various related services and the professionals who serve as related-service providers. While there is no exhaustive list, we group them into categories we've developed over years of conversation with others in education. We hope these categories are helpful to you, as well. Chapters 4 and 5 include some how-to resources David has developed with others as a result of student needs in transportation (chapter 4) and medical/health needs (chapter 5). These are opportunities to walk through a questionnaire/assessment tool for each area, along with some comments and questions to guide your IEP team conversations about these related services. Chapter 6 is the reason Lisa wanted to write this book: to share the value-add related-service providers offer to school communities and IEP teams. This includes what can and should be expected in IEP development and implementation, collaboration within an IEP team and a school team, and from a supervisory perspective. Chapter 7 offers recommendations and resources to explore as you continue your collaborative conversations about how related services support the needs of the students you serve. Finally, the appendices offer information on Supreme Court cases involving related services and three case studies with questions that support connecting the content in this book to your daily work.

Again, thank you for joining us. Let's get started!

Chapter One

Related Services
Definition, Purpose, and Overview

DEFINITION AND PURPOSE OF RELATED SERVICES

Officially, students eligible for special education include those showing a need for special education and related services. The problem is, we too often focus on the *special education* part and forget that many students eligible for special education also need additional services in order to receive a free appropriate public education (FAPE). These additional services are called *related services*. According to federal regulations,

> Related services means transportation and such developmental, corrective, and other supportive services as are required to assist a child with a disability to benefit from special education, and includes speech-language pathology and audiology services, interpreting services, psychological services, physical and occupational therapy, recreation, including therapeutic recreation, early identification and assessment of disabilities in children, counseling services, including rehabilitation counseling, orientation and mobility services, and medical services for diagnostic or evaluation purposes. Related services also include school health services and school nurse services, social work services in schools, and parent counseling and training. (Individuals with Disabilities Education Act, 2006, 34 C.F.R. § 300.34)

This formal definition has a lot to unpack and can feel overwhelming to the reader. A logical first question is, What does it mean? As this book explains, there are some students eligible for special education who need more than what a special education teacher can provide by themselves. To truly benefit from special education services, these students need additional, related services and supports that can only be provided by other professionals. This first chapter provides a broad introduction of related services and how they fit into the individualized education plan (IEP). Again, this is an overview. We provide more detail in later chapters.

RELATED SERVICES AND THE IEP

A student may require any of the following related services in order to benefit from special education. Related services, as listed under the Individuals with Disabilities Education Act (IDEA), include but are not limited to the following:

- Audiology services
- Counseling services
- Early identification and assessment of disabilities in children
- Interpreting services
- Medical services
- Occupational therapy
- Orientation and mobility services
- Parent or guardian counseling and training
- Physical therapy
- Psychological services
- Recreation
- Rehabilitation counseling services
- School health services
- Social work services in schools
- Speech-language pathology services
- Transportation

This list is not exhaustive, and other developmental, corrective, or supportive services may be required to help a student with a disability benefit from special education. Keep in mind that a student with a disability may not require a related service, or the student may require a combination of services. All students should be treated individually, and decisions should be made by the IEP team, utilizing the information from the comprehensive evaluation.

After careful review of a student's evaluation, the IEP team determines the specific related service or services the student is to receive (if any) and includes those services in the student's IEP. If a related service is deemed necessary, then the appropriate related-service professional should be involved in developing the IEP. That individual may be invited by the school or parent/guardian to join the IEP team as a person "with knowledge or special expertise" about the child. We provide more information on related-service providers in chapter 3 and the value-add they bring to the IEP team in chapter 6.

Once the needed related services are identified, goals are written for each related service, just as they are for other special education services. The IEP must also specify the following information for each related service:

- When the service will begin
- How often it will be provided and for what amount of time
- Where it will be provided [Individuals with Disabilities Education Act, 2006, § 300.320(a)(7)]

Once the type and amount of related services are noted in the student's IEP, the school district must ensure that all specified related services are, in fact, provided. Changes in the amount or type of services listed in the IEP cannot be made without another IEP meeting.

There are many factors to consider when examining related services. To support connection and clarification of the information about related services, in Appendix A are three case studies of students who receive a variety of related services: Max, Saraiah, and Angelus. Each case study includes some discussion questions or points to consider. These can be used in your individual learning or as conversation starters while your team is learning together. We hope these connections are as helpful to you as they are to us when we are thinking about how to determine and implement related services to support individual students.

RELATED SERVICES

IDEA stipulates that each child's IEP must contain

> (4) A statement of the special education and related services and supplementary aids and services, based on peer-reviewed research to the extent practicable, to be provided to the child, or on behalf of the child, and a statement of the program modifications or supports for school personnel that will be provided to enable the child—
>
> (i) To advance appropriately toward attaining the annual goals;
>
> (ii) To be involved in and make progress in the general education curriculum in accordance with paragraph (a)(1) of this section, and to participate in extracurricular and other nonacademic activities; and
>
> (iii) To be educated and participate with other children with disabilities and nondisabled children in the activities described in this section. [Individuals with Disabilities Education Act, 2006, § 300.320(a)(4)]

If you're like us, you have questions after reading that riveting section of the law. Let's address some of those questions together.

How?

How does a child become eligible for related services? Like all special education services, it starts with an evaluation. To be eligible for and receive special education and related services, the student must have a full evaluation in all areas of suspected disability. This is often a tricky part for students who are either new to a district or are not yet eligible for special education. Many special services must have special education eligibility and must be indicated as necessary for the student to move forward in the curriculum before the related service can be provided. It does not mean, however, that we cannot give a student more time on an exam or frequent access to the bathroom if they need it; those are items clearly under the purview of the general education teacher. As a part of the evaluation, it is very important to delineate the specifics of the related services that are needed and how much is necessary (more on this later).

What?

What specifically is a related service? Let's make sure that it is clear from the beginning: the extra services we describe are only provided to students eligible for special education. Could others benefit from the various services we list? Absolutely. However, the goal of related services is to assist students with disabilities to benefit from their special education services (that are written into their IEP) by providing extra help and support in needed areas, such as transportation, mobility, or even speaking.

The following is a list of related services a student might receive. This is not a comprehensive list, as the individual needs of the students dictate the services to be provided, *not* what is available (more on this later, too). The savvy reader will notice we mention multiple times that there is not an exhaustive list of related services and that related-service needs are determined by the IEP team on an individual basis for a child. There may be a student in your district with a unique disability and specific needs that must be addressed by related services but does not appear on the following list.

Not Exhaustive yet Alphabetical List of Related Services

- Audiology services
- Counseling services
- Early identification and assessment of disabilities in children
- Interpreting services
- Medical services for diagnostic or evaluation purposes
- Occupational therapy

- Orientation and mobility services
- Parent or guardian counseling and training
- Physical therapy
- Psychological services
- Rehabilitation counseling
- School health and school nurse services
- Social work services
- Speech-language pathology
- Therapeutic recreation

Again, this list is not comprehensive. There may be other services necessary to assist students eligible for special education. And now you know that's because the related-service needs of a student with an IEP are determined on an individualized basis by the IEP team.

When?

A student becomes eligible for a related service *only* after an evaluation declares the student eligible for special education. The evaluation is the gateway for a student to start receiving a related service. The eligibility for the related service does not have to happen solely at the initial evaluation identifying the student eligible for special education. It may occur any time after the student becomes eligible for special education. For example, a student may not need transportation assistance when they first become eligible for special education as an elementary student, but as their physical disability progresses or because of a change in schools, they may later require transportation assistance. This is an important point to remember; the discussion of services a student needs may happen at any time, and IEP teams are strongly encouraged to have this discussion every time the IEP team meets to address the student's program.

Another important component of "when" is how much or how often related services are needed. If you've read this far, then you won't be surprised by this pro tip: The amount of related services a student should receive is dependent on the needs of the student, not on what the district or division has to offer. For example, a student may require transportation assistance to get to and from school, and the typical times that transportation is provided is right before school and at the end of the regularly scheduled school day. However, if the student participates in extracurricular activities after school, then the transportation schedule needs to be modified.

The real answer to the question of when a related services is to be provided is: It depends. It depends on the specific related service(s) the student is to receive. It depends on the specific needs of the student. It may also change over time, as a student's needs might not stay the same. Therefore, there is no specific answer to when or how much of a related service a student is to receive. Determining the extent of need for the student and whether changes are necessary should be a topic of conversation at *every* IEP meeting.

We point this out numerous times throughout this book, but the IEP is a written commitment for the delivery of services to meet a student's educational needs. A school district must ensure that all the related services specified in the IEP, including the amount, are provided to a student. Changes to the amount or frequency of services listed in the IEP cannot be made without holding another IEP meeting. However, if there is no change in the overall amount of service, then some adjustments in the scheduling of services may be possible without another IEP meeting.

Evaluation and Progress Monitoring

Just providing a student a related service, be it speech therapy, handwriting assistance through occupational therapy, or even tutoring, should not be the end of the process for the team. The IEP team should revisit the needs of the student regularly. Even though IEPs are written with annual goals and are expected to be reviewed annually, the IEP team should at a minimum review the progress the student is making at the end of each marking period. This is when grades are reported and updated, and it's the perfect time to connect with the related-service providers to see if the student needs more, less, or the same amount of services. Progress checks or service updates could also occur more frequently if necessary. (Remember: The needs of the student drive the services, not the process or structure the school, district, or division is used to providing.) The progress discussions will ensure the student is receiving the necessary services, and the team can facilitate long-term discussion about the student's progress. Additionally, what may seem good on paper or in a meeting may not be working for the student, and the team may have to revise to ensure the student's needs are being addressed.

The determination that a child needs related services is a team decision. It is not the decision of one individual. The parents or guardians are members of the team, and the decision about related services needs to be made *at* the IEP meeting, not beforehand. IDEA does not require related-service personnel to attend the IEP team meeting, but it is a very good practice, as the individual likely to provide the related service can answer questions and address concerns. Specifically, IDEA states that, at the discretion of the parent/guardian or the public agency, "other individuals who have knowledge or special expertise regarding the child, including related services personnel as appropriate" may be part of a child's IEP team (Individuals with Disabilities Education Act, 2006, § 300.321). Sometimes, being part of the IEP team means providing written input, but having the related-service provider attend the meeting is preferable, especially when discussing related services.

Cost

What is the cost of the related services to the parents or guardians? A related service is a part of the free appropriate public education (FAPE) that a local school district or charter school is obligated to provide. Appendix B includes summaries of two Supreme Court decisions on related services in special education. Each Supreme Court decision makes it abundantly clear that the cost of the services is to be borne by the district, not the parents or guardians. Specifically, services that are not medical in nature are the responsibilities of the district. This is referred to as the "bright line" test.

If a related service is required to enable a student with a disability to remain in school, it must be provided as long as it is not a purely medical service. If the service can only be provided by a licensed physician, then it is an exempt medical service, unless it is needed for diagnostic or evaluative purposes. If, however, the service is capable of being delivered by a nonphysician, then it must be provided by school districts, regardless of any financial or staffing burdens the act of providing the services might impose (Yell, 2019).

Exclusions

Related services encompass a very broad area—one that is dictated by the needs of the student. We later describe in greater detail the most common types of related services. However, it is very important also to address the specific related services that are purposefully excluded from the list. Remember: Related services are only for those students who are eligible for special education. That in and of itself is a potential exclusion from additional services for many students.

An area of exclusion includes the installation of cochlear implants. A cochlear implant is a "small, complex electronic device that can help to provide a sense of sound to a person who is profoundly deaf or severely hard-of-hearing" (National Institute on Deafness and Other Communication Disorders, 2017). Cochlear implants are not the only surgically implanted devices that school districts are *not* responsible for providing. Others include an insulin pump, hearing aids, baclofen pump, pacemaker, G-tube, and vagus nerve stimulator device.

The implantation of these devices is specifically *not* the responsibility of education. However, that does not mean they are to ignore the devices altogether. IDEA regulations specially address the supported services necessary to facilitate the use of these devices [Individuals with Disabilities Education Act, 2006, § 300.34(b)]. School districts specifically are not responsible for optimizing these devices, maintaining them, or replacing them. Even so, school districts are responsible for "routine checking to determine if the external component of a surgically implanted device is turned on and working" (Individuals with Disabilities Education Act, 2006, 71 Fed. Reg. 46570). For example, when working as a speech-language pathologist in a school, Lisa provided daily hearing aid and cochlear implant checks for students. This was a simple check of function: Is the device working? If the device wasn't working properly, then Lisa notified the parent. She was not responsible for maintenance or replacement of the devices. (As a matter of good practice, she also notified the instructors and offered ideas for how to accommodate the student differently to ensure educational activities occurred even if the student was unable to hear at the typical level. This is an example of the collaborative nature and value-add of the related-service provider on the team!)

School districts may be responsible for providing other types of technology services the child needs, as determined by the IEP team, including

- assistive technology,
- air conditioning,
- FM transmitters, and
- proper classroom acoustical modifications.

School districts are not responsible for the mapping of a cochlear implant, but they would be expected to provide the speech-language services necessary for a student who has recently received a cochlear implant. For instance,

> Particularly with younger children or children who have recently obtained implants, teachers and related services personnel frequently are the first to notice changes in the child's perception of sounds that the child may be missing. This may manifest as a lack of attention or understanding on the part of the child or frustration in communicating. The changes may indicate a need for remapping, and we would expect that school personnel would communicate with the child's parents or guardians about these issues. To the extent that adjustments to the devices are required, a specially trained professional would provide the remapping, which is not considered the responsibility of the public agency. (Individuals with Disabilities Education Act, 2006, 71 Fed. Reg. 46570-1)

Schools need to work with students who have recently received a cochlear implant just like they would work with a student who has hearing loss and uses a hearing aid. What distinguishes the difference under the law between the two is that the excluded responsibility is, in large measure, related to the "level of expertise required." Maintaining and monitoring a surgically implanted device requires the expertise of a licensed physician or an individual with specialized technical expertise beyond that typically available from school personnel.

As described in this example, if a teacher notices that a student is unable to participate or cannot hear due to a malfunctioning hearing aid or cochlear implant, then it is the school's responsibility to alert the parents or guardians of such and encourage them to meet with the medical provider(s). IDEA notes public agencies remain aware of and responsible for monitoring and maintaining "medical devices that are needed to maintain the health and safety of the child, including breathing, nutrition, or operation of other bodily functions, while the child is transported to and from school or is at school" [Individuals with Disabilities Education Act, 2006, § 300.34(b)(2)(ii)].

SPECIFIC RELATED SERVICES

The following is a list and brief description of specific related services that are defined in the regulations. Remember: There may be related services students need that are not on this list. The needs of the student dictate the services to be provided. Think of this list as a slightly expanded version of a "Not Exhaustive yet Alphabetical" quick reference guide for related services.

Art Therapy

Art therapy is a distinct discipline that incorporates creative methods of expression through visual art media. It provides individuals with disabilities with a means of self-expression and opportunities to expand personal creativity and control. By involving students with art and the creative art process, art therapists work to help students address their unique needs, which may include resolving emotional conflicts, developing self-awareness or social skills, managing behavior, solving problems, reducing anxiety, and improving self-esteem.

Assistive Technology

Assistive technology service is "any service that directly assists a child with a disability in the selection, acquisition, or use of an assistive technology device" (Individuals with Disabilities Education Act, 2006, § 300.6). School districts are responsible for helping individuals with disabilities select and acquire appropriate assistive-technology devices and train them in their use if doing so is necessary for them to receive FAPE (Individuals with Disabilities Education Act, 2006, § 300.308). Such services include

a. The evaluation of the needs of a child with a disability, including a functional evaluation in the child's customary environment;
b. Purchasing, leasing, or otherwise providing for the acquisition of assistive technology devices by children with disabilities;
c. Selecting, designing, fitting, customizing, adapting, applying, maintaining, repairing, or replacing assistive technology devices;
d. Coordinating and using other therapies, interventions, or services with assistive technology devices, such as those associated with existing education and rehabilitation plans and programs;
e. Training or technical assistance for a child with a disability or, if appropriate, the child's family; and
f. Training or technical assistance for professionals (including individuals providing education or rehabilitation services), employers, or other individuals who provide services to, employ, or are substantially involved in the major functions of that child. (Individuals with Disabilities Education Act, 2006, § 300.6)

Assistive technology is becoming an increasingly used related service but like the others must be individualized to the needs of the student, not the disability label, and must be periodically evaluated to determine whether it is effective.

Audiology Services

Audiology services include the following:

i. Identification of children with hearing loss;
ii. Determination of the range, nature, and degree of hearing loss, including referral for medical or other professional attention for the habilitation of hearing;
iii. Provision of habilitative activities, such as language habilitation, auditory training, speech reading (lip-reading), hearing evaluation, and speech conservation;

iv. Creation and administration of programs for prevention of hearing loss;
v. Counseling and guidance of children, parents, and teachers regarding hearing loss; and
vi. Determination of children's needs for group and individual amplification, selecting and fitting an appropriate aid, and evaluating the effectiveness of amplification. [Individuals with Disabilities Education Act, 2006, § 300.34(c)(1)]

This service supports students with hearing loss by determining the range, nature, and degree of a child's hearing loss and both group and individual needs for amplification. If there is not a diagnostic facility within a school district, then the district must contract with another agency to help diagnose the hearing loss.

Counseling Services

Counseling services are "provided by qualified social workers, psychologists, guidance counselors, or other qualified personnel" [Individuals with Disabilities Education Act, 2006, § 300.34(c)(2)]. Counseling services can include helping children with personal and social concerns, such as developing self-knowledge, making effective decisions, learning health choices, and improving responsibility. Counselors also may help children with future planning related to setting and reaching academic goals, developing a positive attitude toward learning, and recognizing and using academic strengths.

There are additional counseling services defined by IDEA, such as parent/guardian counseling and rehabilitation counseling. Counseling services are different from psychological services.

Early Identification and Assessment of Disabilities in Children

Early identification and assessment of disabilities in children is the "implementation of a formal plan for identifying a disability as early as possible in a child's life" [Individuals with Disabilities Education Act, 2006, § 300.34(c)(3)]. This is an individual service for one child. If a child's IEP team determines that identifying and assessing the nature of a child's disability is necessary for the child to benefit from their special education, then this related service must be listed in the child's IEP and provided to the child. The team would then develop a formal plan to establish the process and procedures by which the child's disability will be identified.

Interpreting Services

Interpreting services are defined as

   i. The following, when used with respect to children who are deaf or hard of hearing: Oral transliteration services, cued language transliteration services, sign language transliteration and interpreting services, and transcription services, such as communication access real-time translation (CART), C-Print, and TypeWell; and
  ii. Special interpreting services for children who are deaf-blind. [Individuals with Disabilities Education Act, 2006, § 300.34(c)(4)]

This is not a new service. It has previously been provided to students who are deaf or hard of hearing but expands on opportunities for others. It can include oral transliteration and cued language.

Occupational Therapy

IDEA § 300.34(c)(6) defines *occupational therapy* (OT) as

   i. ... services provided by a qualified occupational therapist; and
  ii. Includes—
      a. Improving, developing, or restoring functions impaired or lost through illness, injury, or deprivation;
      b. Improving ability to perform tasks for independent functioning if functions are impaired or lost; and
      c. Preventing, through early intervention, initial or further impairment or loss of function.

OT services can enhance a child's ability to function in an educational program and may help with self-help skills or adaptive living; functional mobility; positioning; sensory-motor processing; and fine motor and, to a lesser extent, gross motor performance. It is a common related service.

Orientation and Mobility Services

IDEA § 300.34(c)(7) states that orientation and mobility services

   i. Means services provided to blind or visually impaired children by qualified personnel to enable those students to attain systematic orientation to and safe movement within their environments in school, home, and community; and

ii. Includes teaching children the following, as appropriate:
   a. Spatial and environmental concepts and use of information received by the senses (such as sound, temperature and vibrations) to establish, maintain, or regain orientation and line of travel (e.g., using sound at a traffic light to cross the street);
   b. To use the long cane or a service animal to supplement visual travel skills or as a tool for safely negotiating the environment for children with no available travel vision;
   c. To understand and use remaining vision and distance low vision aids; and
   d. Other concepts, techniques, and tools.

Abbreviated as O&M, these services are designed explicitly for students with vision impairments.

Parent/Guardian Counseling and Training

Parent/guardian counseling and training is defined as

i. ... assisting parents in understanding the special needs of their child;
ii. Providing parents with information about child development; and
iii. Helping parents to acquire the necessary skills that will allow them to support the implementation of their child's IEP or IFSP. [Individuals with Disabilities Education Act, 2006, § 300.34(c)(8)]

Parent/guardian counseling and training can help parents or guardians enhance the vital role they play in the lives of their children. Parent/guardian counseling and training would only be provided to parents or guardians if a child's IEP team determines that it is necessary for the child to receive FAPE.

Physical Therapy

Physical therapy is defined as "services provided by a qualified physical therapist" [Individuals with Disabilities Education Act, 2006, § 300.34(c)(9)]. These services generally address a child's posture, muscle strength, mobility, and organization of movement in educational environments.

Psychological Services

Psychological services are defined as

i. Administering psychological and educational tests, and other assessment procedures;
ii. Interpreting assessment results;
iii. Obtaining, integrating, and interpreting information about child behavior and conditions relating to learning;
iv. Consulting with other staff members in planning school programs to meet the special educational needs of children as indicated by psychological tests, interviews, direct observation, and behavioral evaluations;
v. Planning and managing a program of psychological services, including psychological counseling for children and parents; and
vi. Assisting in developing positive behavioral intervention strategies. [Individuals with Disabilities Education Act, 2006, § 300.34(c)(10)]

These services are delivered to help eligible children with disabilities benefit from their special education. They may be provided by a school psychologist, school social workers, or school counselors.

Recreation

Recreation services are defined as

i. Assessment of leisure function;
ii. Therapeutic recreation services;
iii. Recreation programs in schools and community agencies; and
iv. Leisure education. [Individuals with Disabilities Education Act, 2006, § 300.34(c)(11)]

Through these services, children can learn appropriate and functional recreation and leisure skills.

Rehabilitation Counseling

Rehabilitation counseling is defined as

> services provided by qualified personnel in individual or group sessions that focus specifically on career development, employment preparation, achieving independence, and integration in the workplace and community of a student with a disability. The term also includes vocational rehabilitation services provided to a student with a disability by vocational rehabilitation programs funded under the Rehabilitation Act of 1973, as amended, 29 U.S.C. 701 et seq. [Individuals with Disabilities Education Act, 2006, § 300.34(c)(12)]

Every state has a central vocational rehabilitation (VR) agency, along with many local offices. Often, VR providers are invited to IEP team meetings for high school students to discuss transition and vocational services needed to support transition goals.

School Health and School Nurse Services

School health and school nurse services are defined as "health services that are designed to enable a child with a disability to receive FAPE as described in the child's IEP. School nurse services are services provided by a qualified school nurse. School health services are services that may be provided by either a qualified school nurse or other qualified person" [Individuals with Disabilities Education Act, 2006, §300.34(c)(13)]. Please read the *Tatro* and *Garret F.* Supreme Court decisions (Appendix B) on the bright-line test between medical versus health services. Possible health services include

- special feedings;
- cleaning intermittent catheterization;
- suctioning;
- managing a tracheostomy;
- administering and/or dispensing medications;
- planning for the safety of a child in school;
- ensuring that care is given while at school and at school functions to prevent injury (e.g., changing a child's position frequently to prevent pressure sores);
- managing chronic disease; and
- conducting and/or promoting education and skills training for all (including the child) who serve as caregivers in the school setting.

Social Work Services in Schools

Social work services are defined as

i. Preparing a social or developmental history on a child with a disability;
ii. Group and individual counseling with the child and family;
iii. Working in partnership with parents and others on those problems in a child's living situation (home, school, and community) that affect the child's adjustment in school;
iv. Mobilizing school and community resources to enable the child to learn as effectively as possible in his or her educational program; and

v. Assisting in developing positive behavioral intervention strategies. [Individuals with Disabilities Education Act, 2006, § 300.34(c)(14)]

The problems many students experienced as a result of COVID-19 highlighted the importance of addressing the needs of the student in all areas. This can often be done with the assistance of a social worker.

Speech-Language Pathology

Speech-language pathology is defined as

i. Identification of children with speech or language impairments;
ii. Diagnosis and appraisal of specific speech or language impairments;
iii. Referral for medical or other professional attention necessary for the habilitation of speech or language impairments;
iv. Provision of speech and language services for the habilitation or prevention of communicative impairments; and
v. Counseling and guidance of parents, children, and teachers regarding speech and language impairments. [Individuals with Disabilities Education Act, 2006, § 300.34(c)(15)]

This is one of the most common related services for eligible students. It is also the only related service that can be a sole eligibility service provided to students. This means that there are some students who are eligible for special education solely because of a need for speech-language service. These services should be provided by (or supervised by) a licensed and certified speech-language pathologist.

Transportation

Transportation is defined as

i. Travel to and from school and between schools;
ii. Travel in and around school buildings; and
iii. Specialized equipment (such as special or adapted buses, lifts, and ramps), if required to provide special transportation for a child with a disability. [Individuals with Disabilities Education Act, 2006, § 300.34(c)(17)]

Transportation is included in an eligible child's IEP if the IEP team determines that such a service is needed for the child to benefit from their special education. Transportation as a related service may also mean providing modifications and supports so that a child may ride the regular school bus used in transporting children without disabilities (Individuals with Disabilities Education Act, 2006, 71 Fed. Reg. 46576).

Not all children with disabilities are eligible to receive transportation as a related service. A child's need for transportation as a related service and the type of transportation to be provided must be discussed and decided by the IEP team. If the IEP team determines the eligible student needs transportation to benefit from their special education, then it should be included in the IEP.

IMPORTANT AND CONNECTED POINTS

This chapter provides an overview of related services and may have generated additional questions for you. That's great! We continue exploring more about related services and related-service providers but want to point out a few connected points:

- With appropriate supports, most students with disabilities can be successful in the general education classroom; some students, however, may need supports that are more intensive than what can be provided by a general education teacher. This is why decisions about special education services, related services, and least restrictive environment (LRE) are made during the IEP team meeting and specifically for that individual student.
- Many students in special education receive related services that are necessary to help them benefit from special education services.
- Special education services and related services may be provided in a general education setting or a special education setting or both. There are many ways we can help students receive special education supports in the general education classroom. Again, the IEP team should determine how, when, and where the services are provided.
- It is important for teachers to work closely with paraprofessionals, who provide important assistance for some students with disabilities. While outside the scope of this chapter, information on paraprofessionals can be found in the resources at the end of this book.
- Sometimes general education teachers work with outside service providers to address student needs. (See the examples in this chapter.)

SUMMARY AND KEY POINTS

This chapter defines *related services* and which students are eligible for these services, describes the process through which they are determined, and provides examples. As you review this information and connect it to the case studies in Appendix A, it is important to understand these key points:

- Related services are based on the individual needs of the student, not on what is currently available through the school district or division.
- The list of related services in this chapter is based on the federal regulations. There may be other services necessary for a child to receive a free appropriate public education.
- The decision about the necessary related services to be provided is made by the student's IEP team, and those services must be included in the student's IEP.
- Students need to be eligible for special education in order to receive related services.
- Related services are provided at no cost to the parents or guardians.
- The related service needs to be periodically reevaluated to determine if it is addressing the specific needs of the student.

ACTIVE LEARNING ENGAGEMENT

1. In the section on cost, we mention the two Supreme Court cases that involve related services. You can find summaries of these cases and some questions to consider in Appendix B.
2. As you reflect on the types of related services that are available, check your knowledge and understanding with the case studies of Max, Saraiah, and Angelus in Appendix A. Each example includes questions to consider that can be used for self-check or in professional-development exercises with your school team.

KEY TERMS

assistive technology (AT): a device or service used by individuals with disabilities to assist with functions that might be difficult. Walkers, wheelchairs, screen readers, picture-exchange communication systems, and magnifying devices are all considered assistive technology.
bright-line test: a clearly stated and easy-to-follow rule.
free appropriate public education (FAPE): the education to which every student is entitled under IDEA. Every student is entitled to an education that is appropriate for their unique needs and that is provided at no cost to the parents or guardians.

individualized education program (IEP): a legal document between the school district and the parents or guardians that defines special education services for an individual child eligible to receive special education; also individualized education plan.

Individuals with Disabilities Education Act (IDEA): a law that guarantees educational rights to all students with disabilities and makes it illegal for school districts to refuse to educate a student based on their disability.

medical services: services that can only be provided by a licensed physician; exempt from the definition of *related services* unless needed for diagnostic or evaluative purposes.

progress monitoring: scheduled data collection to monitor a student's progress toward a goal.

regulations: instructions written by the executive branch that provide direction on how to implement and enforce laws passed by Congress. Special educators must be aware of federal and state regulations pertaining to special education law.

related services: transportation and such developmental, corrective, and other supportive services required to help a child with a disability benefit from special education.

special education: education specially designed to meet the unique needs of a child with a disability.

QUESTIONS TO CONSIDER

1. What is the definition of *related services*?
2. How does this definition affect your understanding of the related services provided in your school, district, or division?
3. In your own words, how would you describe the difference between related services and special education?
4. What is a bright-line test, and why is it important for related services?
5. How are related services determined in a student's IEP?
6. Finish this sentence: The amount of the related service provided to a student is dependent on _____.
7. What are the school's responsibilities in supporting a student with medical needs that require a physician?

Chapter Two

Requirements and Considerations of Related Services

The first chapter provides an overview of related services, with definitions and basic regulations. This chapter delves into greater detail about the IEP process—how related services should be determined and incorporated into the student's IEP. The following sections use the federal regulations as guidance about the requirements for working with students with disabilities as a part of their IEP. Your state may have slightly different rules or requirements on the actual implementation of the services, but what we provide here is a broad overview that will help any teacher and service provider identify what should be done.

Why are there slightly different rules or requirements across states? While IDEA is a federal law with federal regulations, each state is tasked with implementing this law. As a result, state regulations may differ slightly in wording and focus. This results in some nuanced differences across states, so it's good to know both the federal law (IDEA) and how your state addresses those federal requirements through state regulations. Each district should have a special education administrator who is responsible for ensuring the district is adhering to the state and federal regulations.

SPECIFICS RELATED TO THE IEP

The purpose of developing a meaningful and legally sound IEP is to enable eligible students to make progress. There are two important components to that sentence: The IEP must be meaningful (enable the student to make progress) and legally sound (meet the legal requirements of IDEA). Because educators must collaboratively develop IEPs that are meaningful and enable students to make progress while being legally sound, we offer a method of

IEP development that is legally sound and relies on better practices. Using better practices in an IEP may go beyond what the law actually requires, but the use of such practices will enable special educators to meet the legal requirements while developing and implementing special education programs that enable students to make progress in light of their unique educational needs. Although we do not offer legal advice, we believe the better practices we propose will assist special educators to develop and implement IEPs that meet both requirements. To learn more about the requirements of meaningful goals that are legally sound, check out the resources in chapter 7.

We recognize this chapter feels a little heavy and can be intimidating at first, as it involves some legal components of IEPs, so we break this chapter into sections. We start our discussion with 12 tips when considering related services for eligible students. Each tip—based on the regulations and providing guidance for the IEP team—can be reviewed individually to facilitate connection, considerations, and conversations. We then clarify the various purposes of the IEP, as well as the required components of the IEP document. We discuss the various roles of the IEP team members, as well as provide a summary of a typical IEP meeting. We wrap up with four important IEP points for classroom teachers. As with every chapter, we also offer some questions to consider to extend your thinking. It is our hope that some of this feels like review for you, while other parts may help fill in gaps or answer questions for you and your team.

12 IEP TIPS

Tip 1

IDEA provides a definition of *related services* and lists of a number of possible related services, such as speech, occupational therapy, physical therapy, counseling, transportation, and parent training [Individuals with Disabilities Education Act, 2006, 34 C.F.R. Section 300.34(a)]. Remember that this list is not exhaustive and only lists some examples of related services. Other services may qualify as related services even if they are not listed in the federal definition.

Tip 2

Related services are provided under IDEA when the student is identified with a disability and receives special education services and the related service is required to be added to the IEP in order for the student to make progress. Related services are not provided under IDEA unless the student qualifies for special education services (see *Irving Independent School District v. Tatro*, 1984). Basically, the IEP team must find that the particular related service is necessary for a free and appropriate public education (FAPE) and in support of the special education services required by the student.

Tip 3

Services provided by a doctor are medical services and are *not* required as a related service (*Cedar Rapids Community School District v. Garret F.*, 1999). Services provided by a nurse, if required for the student with disabilities to attend school, may qualify as a related service.

Tip 4

The cost of the related service is not part of the definition of a related service. This includes what some districts may consider as costly nursing services. If the student needs them to make progress and attend school, then they may be a related service and are not excluded as a medical service. All needed related services are to be provided at no cost to the parents or guardians.

Tip 5

Related services are not provided just because a doctor, treating psychiatrist, or psychologist has prescribed the service for the child with a disability. The information provided by the professional must be fully considered, but the recommendation is not determinative of the need for the related service. This is an IEP team decision.

Tip 6

The need for related services under IDEA is determined by the IEP team. It is the IEP team who discusses and decides the need for a particular related service. Therefore, a school district should not use the eligibility process to determine if the student qualifies for a related service.

Tip 7

Most related services would be beneficial for any student, but that does not mean all students are eligible for them. The test for the provision of related services is not whether they are beneficial but whether they are needed for FAPE. Therefore, do not focus the IEP discussion about a related service solely on the benefit that the student will receive from the provision of the related service. Focus the discussion on the need for the related service in conjunction with the provision of FAPE.

Tip 8

It is very important that related-service personnel document the provision of the related service and the amount specified in the IEP. As a result, it is important to keep track of the provision of the related services to ensure compliance with the IEP. Related-service providers should be involved in the development—and implementation—of the IEP.

Tip 9

The related-service provider must document the implementation of related-service goals and objectives and the collection of data or information so that progress reports can be provided to parents or guardians. This is yet another reason the related-service provider should be involved in the IEP team.

Tip 10

The related-service provider should be invited to the IEP meeting in many cases so that the IEP team has the information needed about the amount of related service(s) to provide and the corresponding goals. However, the related-service provider is not a required participant in the IEP meeting. If the related-service provider is not present at the IEP meeting, then the IEP team must be prepared to discuss related services by being knowledgeable about the student's continued need for and current performance in the area of the related service.

Tip 11

The related service listed in the IEP needs to be provided from Day 1 of the school year. Do not wait 2 weeks to learn the schedule, await other information, and so on. Develop a plan for providing the service from the beginning of the school year.

Tip 12

Finally and most importantly, the amount of related service a student with disabilities receives is not determined by the schedule or workload of the related-service provider. Please make sure that statements are not made at the

IEP meeting suggesting that decisions are based on staff availability rather than on the student's individual needs.

CLARITY ON THE SERVICES PROVIDED

As you can see from these tips, it is very important to keep the team aware of the specifics of the services to be provided to the student. The IEP is essentially a contract between the school district and the parents or guardians listing specifically the services that will be provided to the student. It is *not* a lesson plan but a rough road map of what services and supports the district will provide to the student in the next year. Given that it is a road map, the IEP serves multiple purposes that need to be explained.

IEP Purposes

The IEP document itself is very important for listing the related services provided. It is where the IEP team documents the plan they have developed to support the student. This document can be used for several purposes. They are not necessarily separate from each other, and in many ways, they are linked together.

Communication

The IEP document is a tool for all team members, including the parents or guardians, to refer to as a reminder of the agreed-upon plan. The IEP document also serves as a tool for the multidisciplinary team to communicate to the rest of the education professionals the specific related services and supports the student is expected to receive and outlines who is responsible for which services.

Annual Performance Goals

IEPs list goals and objectives that should be reasonable for the student to achieve over the next year. These goals are based on the student's present level of functioning and will drive the special educational services for the student.

Services Provided

Specific services a student is to receive are listed in the IEP. If the student is expected to receive speech-language instruction by a speech-language pathologist, then the instruction would be listed in the IEP, along with the frequency and duration of the services. If the student is expected to receive 30 minutes of instruction/consultation from an occupational therapist or if a student were to receive special services for transportation to and from school, then these would be outlined in the IEP document.

Evaluation

The IEP document also allows the IEP team to determine if the student needs the specific related services. For each related service, the IEP documents the student's current level of functioning and needs based on that level. Parents or guardians are to be regularly informed about the student's progress and needs throughout the school year. The following year, when a new IEP is written, the student's level of function is again documented. It should then be easy to see the improvement in functioning when comparing the IEP year to year.

Management

As a management tool, the administrators will be able to refer to this document when they are planning the allocation of staff and resources. Some students may require extensive related services in order to function in schools, while others may require only minimal supports. The administrators need to allocate district resources to ensure these services are provided. The IEP document is a tool they can rely on to help them plan appropriately. Related-service providers are also able to use the document as a management tool. The IEP document will help the provider(s) plan for the amount of instructional time necessary to assist a student, as well as set up the instruction and intervention methods, materials, and space to meet the student's needs.

Accountability

The district needs to ensure the program the IEP team developed and agreed on is implemented, and the IEP document assists with that. Related services are written into the IEP, and the district is expected to make a good-faith effort to ensure that a student receives these services. This, in part, holds the district accountable. If the student does not make progress on the written goals, then the district should reconvene the IEP team to change either the level of supports provided to a student or the specific goals they are addressing. These decisions to make changes to the IEP must be made by the team and based on quality information regarding student progress.

Compliance and Monitoring

Because districts receive state and federal funding for special education programs, there is a compliance-monitoring process in place to ensure the school district is complying with state and federal regulations regarding the related services for students with disabilities. During this monitoring, the IEP document will be reviewed and will document if these regulations are being met. It is important to keep in mind that if a district is found to be out of compliance with the regulations, then there may be legal consequences.

Contract

The IEP is a legally binding document and should be viewed as a contract between the school district and the parents or guardians. Schools must follow what is written in the IEP; for example, if the IEP team determined a student needs a related service, such as special transportation to and from school, then it would be listed in the IEP, and a school district must provide it. If that does not happen, then the district would be violating the contract and giving the parents or guardians rights to contest it. The same goes if a student is expected to receive any other related service or if the school district is only providing it occasionally. Should the district fail to provide what is listed in the IEP, the parents or guardians can file litigation to get back services provided. School districts are required to provide parents or guardians with a copy of their parental rights each year. This literature lets them know how to exercise their rights to make sure the provisions of the IEP are being implemented as required.

Contracts can change, as long as both parties (school district and parents or guardians) agree to the changes. If there is no agreement to make changes, then the contract as originally written stands, and there can be no changes unless a court rules otherwise.

Required IEP Components

The following sections list the components of the IEP and provide the rationale for each component. Your state may have components different from what are listed here, but this is what most states require. The sections may also be called different names, but they serve the same purpose. Even though this information pertains to all IEPs and this book is specifically about related services, all IEP team members should know these required components, and it doesn't hurt to have a reminder here. Plus, there are some pieces that are especially important for the IEP team to consider when related-service providers are part of the team.

Demographics

This section lists identifying information about the student, which may include name; date of birth; age; grade; disability category; anticipated year of graduation; school district (both local and attending); and parent or guardian names, addresses, and contact information.

IEP Team Signatures

This section is where the IEP team will sign that they were in attendance or participated in the IEP meeting. Some team members, including related-service providers, may participate by providing written information to be shared at the meeting. When the signatures are obtained can vary across states. Some states have IEP team members sign at the beginning of the meeting as an attendance certificate; others sign at the end indicating approval. Make sure you are aware of the practices for your state and district.

Notice of Procedural Safeguards

Parents or guardians are to be provided a copy of the procedural notice, clarifying their rights, at least once a year. This is a place where they can sign, attesting they have received a copy. It is important to get the parents or guardians to sign and date that they have received a copy of this notice so the district has complied with this requirement. The legal requirement is to provide access to the procedural rights, not to ensure parents or guardians understand them. However, as discussed about better practices earlier in this chapter, it is the better practice for the IEP team members to be aware of the procedural rights and support parents or guardians in accessing the information needed to understand their rights.

Special Considerations

There are several questions that must be asked as a part of the IEP. If any of these questions are answered in the affirmative, then there must be programming related to that issue included in the IEP. These questions are often done at the very first part of the meeting and often are dispensed with rather quickly, including:

1. Is the student blind or visually impaired?
2. Is the student deaf or hard of hearing?
3. Does the student have communication needs?
4. Does the student require assistive technology devices or services?

5. Does the student have limited English proficiency?
6. Does the student exhibit behaviors that impede their learning or that of others?

While it can be common practice to move through these questions quickly if the answers allow it, the IEP team should recognize when there has been a change in response and ensure the subsequent IEP document addresses the student's needs.

Present Levels of Academic Achievement and Functional Performance (PLAAFP)

Some states call this the "Present Levels" section or the "Present Level of Educational Performance" section, or PLEP. This section of the IEP document drives the implementation and development of the IEP, goals, special education services, and determination of the need for related services. The PLAAFP provides a summary of the student's performance in their current educational program and indicates the student's instructional and functional levels. It includes information regarding classroom performance and the results of any academic achievement or functional performance assessments that have been administered. Information contained in this section provides baseline data for developing the IEP and the requisite related services. The information in this section should consider the most recent results of the multidisciplinary team report, curriculum-based assessments, and ongoing progress monitoring; why it is important that the student improve in this area; and how their performance compares to that of their peers. The information should be stated in clear and concrete terminology. The following may be included in a statement of present level of performance, and additional detail regarding baseline, current, and future desired performance (which inform the goals) would be expected:

- Student uses a walker when moving around the school.
- Student has difficulty with pencil grasp.
- Student can type 10 letters a minute.
- Student needs behavioral support.

Goals and Objectives

Annual goals are measurable statements describing reasonable expectations of what a student should be able to accomplish over a calendar year. These statements include specifics about the behaviors you want the student to perform (reading, math, handwriting, speech, etc.) and how well you want the student to perform these actions. Many teams use a structure, such as the ABCD-T method (Goran et al., 2020), to ensure all parts of the IEP goal are included. There needs to be a clear and direct link between the student's PLAAFP statement and the goals and objectives.

The IEP team should only write goals and objectives relating to areas where special education is needed. It is not necessary to write goals and objectives for areas in the general education curriculum for which the student is not expected to receive special education. Additionally, the IEP should include how often progress is monitored and how often the reports will be provided to the parents or guardians on the status of the goals and objectives. Parents or guardians need to receive progress notes on the IEP goals at least as often as general education parents and guardians receive report cards. Related-service providers are included on the IEP team and often serve students in multiple buildings or districts, so it is important for the IEP team to ensure they know the reporting schedule for this student.

Supports for the General Education Teacher in the IEP

General education teachers who provide instruction to students with a disability may need assistance in implementing and working with the related-services part of the IEP. For example, the teacher may be responsible for implementing or reinforcing practices related to physical therapy goals, providing (and data-monitoring) reading interventions, or implementing the vision-related accommodations listed in the IEP. This section of the IEP provides an opportunity for the team to discuss and articulate those specific supports or training necessary for school personnel to provide FAPE. Specific supports and training could include:

- adult support/aides—learning aides or behavioral tracking aides provided to help the student to make it through the day;
- resource materials—reading materials, journal articles, or a list of websites that would help the teacher understand the student's disability and how to work more effectively with the student;
- training—workshops on behavior management, new reading techniques, or new ways on how to take data and progress-monitor student performance; and
- equipment—data-tracking software, apps for mobile devices that take data, or adaptive equipment that helps the student participate in the classroom.

For each related service, the IEP should list the needed support(s), the school personnel to receive the support, and location and the frequency of the support to be provided. Location refers to where school personnel will receive the support. Frequency refers to how often school personnel will receive the support. The projected beginning date and the anticipated duration of the support must be listed. Duration refers to the anticipated ending date for support. This feels a bit like the section in the IEP where you list the services the student needs, but this section focuses on *what the school personnel need* in order to provide the services as listed in the IEP.

Extended School Year (ESY)

Extended school year (ESY) includes individualized services to help a child maintain skills and not lose progress made toward goals when there is an extended break in the school year, such as summer (Morin, 2014). Not all students with IEPs receive ESY. The student's IEP team determines the need for ESY services, and ESY services are typically provided during the summer but can be an extension of the student's normal school day, such as a special tutoring program. An important point: If a student requires related services during the school year, then they are likely going to require related services in the ESY program.

This section lists the steps the IEP team will consider in determining a student's eligibility for ESY services. ESY is only for students eligible for special education, and it is only to help students maintain skills, not to advance beyond what they have learned during the school year. ESY is not the same as other summer programs offered to nondisabled students but is specific to the maintenance of IEP goals. It is not mandatory that students attend ESY services. If a student requires a related service during the school year, then the team needs to review whether the related service is necessary for the summer programming.

Placement

The needs of the student determine both the type(s) of related services that must be provided and the location(s) where those services occur. The IEP team and professional related-service providers determine the location of the related services the student is to receive. Related services can be provided in the general education classroom; in the special education classroom; as pull-out services; as push-in services; and even during community-based activities, such as when a class is practicing vocational skills in another setting. Special education is a service, not a place, and the IEP team determines the placement or location for the services based on the student's needs, not on what is administratively available.

Least Restrictive Environment

Least restrictive environment (LRE) is one of the defining parts of IDEA and a main factor for special education. Under LRE, the presumption is students with disabilities will be educated in general education classrooms alongside their typically learning peers to the maximum extent possible and provided with the necessary supports and services to meet their needs. Students with disabilities are to participate fully, both academically and socially. In addition, the general education teacher is expected to differentiate the methods used in the provision of services so all students will benefit from instruction. This also applies to related services. The purpose of LRE is to ensure the student receives an appropriate education in the least restrictive placement possible and is not removed to a more restrictive placement and thus experience discrimination.

Students with disabilities are to be educated in the general education classroom until all available methods are tried to meet their needs in this environment. Only after every reasonable method is tried in the general education classroom and the needs of a student are still not met should the student be pulled out for additional services. Again, this applies to related services, as well.

Examples of this include students with disabilities being briefly removed to receive individualized speech-language therapy and then going back to the general education classroom to allow for opportunity to generalize the targeted skill while engaging in the general education content and curriculum. Another example is students with emotional issues being taught strategies for dealing with frustration by the school psychologist and then going back to the general education classroom for content instruction.

LRE does not include placing a student in a special education class without trying accommodations first or automatically assuming they need assistance just because of their disability. Case law on this is very specific: Removal to a special education classroom is only done after other options have been tried.

Reevaluation

IEP teams must consider if a reevaluation is needed at least once every three years or more frequently if needed or if the parent/guardian or teacher requests it. The reevaluation has three purposes:

1. To determine whether the student remains eligible for special education and related services. (This is the primary purpose.)
2. To ensure the individual needs of a student with a disability are identified.
3. To gather necessary information for appropriate educational programming.

However, it is important to remember that if a reevaluation is completed for any of these reasons, then the team must consider if the student continues to meet the disability category, which is necessary for the student to receive related services. The decision must be documented. The team may determine that more testing is necessary to help make this determination, or they may decide additional information is needed for program planning and not have to go through the formal reevaluation process. You need to check with your special education administrator or special education teacher to see how this is handled in your state and district. Either way, the reevaluation should review and consider evaluations and information provided by the student's parents or guardians, classroom-based assessments and observations, observations by teachers and related-service providers, results of state and district assessments, and comments and data from related-service providers.

The reevaluation process involves the entire IEP team, including the general education teacher. In fact, the general education teacher role includes four important aspects:

1. Share current classroom-based assessments and observations.
2. Share observations of working with teachers and related-service providers.
3. Share any other information pertinent to the reevaluation process (e.g., attendance, health/medical reports, disciplinary record).
4. Clarify, from their perspective, if they still think the student has a disability, how they relate to the other students in the class, and whether the related services are necessary.

Many students will have more than one general education teacher, so the IEP team will want to gather information on these four aspects from as many of them as possible. This is a great example of the importance of the IEP team having a clear communication plan, the need for collaboration between classroom teachers and related-service providers, and the recognition that some team members will provide written input to be considered but will not necessarily attend every meeting.

IEP Team Member with Typical Roles

As mentioned previously, the IEP is a team effort, and there can be quite a few members of the team. Some of these are required by IDEA, some are included as "better practice," and some may have a dual role:

Student: Helps to identify their unique needs and areas where they need support. Not typically required until age 16 (in some states, it is age 14). It is good practice to include them in at least parts of the meeting prior to the required age.

Parent(s)/Guardian(s): Offer important insight(s) on how the student is performing outside the school setting; information on the student's strengths, interests, and concerns in settings outside school; and descriptions of the student's attitude toward school and homework. They can also be an important liaison with outside service providers.

General Education Teacher: Provides valuable insight on expectations for the student regarding the standard curriculum, interactions with other students, the daily schedule, other interventions, and the need for special education and may serve as an important communication point for related-service providers. The general education teacher should consider themselves as the curriculum expert on the team. They will give invaluable information regarding the curriculum taught in their class, the accommodations and modifications that may be needed, the social interactions of the student across school settings, how this student's performance compares to peers, and what specific skills are imperative for the student to learn for them to be successful in the general education setting or to move forward in the curriculum. It cannot be overstated that the role of the general education classroom teacher is important for making sure the student gets the special education and related services they need.

Special Education Teacher: Discusses instructional strategies, adaptations, and the amount of time necessary to implement the goals and can often describe the need for and time commitment necessary for related services. The special educator assigned as the student's case manager typically writes the IEP document. They gather and compile information from team members and complete the IEP to ensure all required components are documented. In some districts, a special education administrator is responsible for the finalized IEP document.

Local Education Agency (LEA) Representative: This is likely a principal or administrator. The LEA is familiar with resources available at other agencies and is able to commit resources to meet IEP goals. The LEA should be familiar with the related-service providers in the area and how they interact with other students in the school.

Person Qualified to Interpret Instructional Implications of Evaluation Results: This is likely a school psychologist or educational diagnostician. This IEP team member interprets the evaluations for designing instructional goals and objectives for the student, determines what accommodations or modifications might be necessary for the student, and is familiar with any related-service needs.

For students who need related services, the related-service providers are also important to have at an IEP meeting. For example, if a student receives physical therapy, then the physical therapist should be part of the IEP team. If the student has hearing loss and requires the use of amplification devices (FM system, hearing aids, etc.), then the audiologist should be part of the IEP team. If the student receives transportation as a related service, then the person responsible for transportation should be at the meeting. It is important to remind the team that the determination of the need for related services is an individual one; it is not based on the child's disability, nor is it based on the specific service(s) the district happens to have or is familiar with providing. The needs of the student dictate the necessary related services. We cover this in more depth in chapter 1 and provide case studies in Appendix A to extend your learning and allow you practice applying the information to student scenarios.

SUMMARY OF A TYPICAL IEP MEETING

The following is a summary of a typical IEP meeting. The actual order of topics may vary from state to state and from district to district, based on the specific requirements and forms used, but the topics and considerations are legally required components of the process, and decisions must be based on the needs of the student:

Introductions: Prior to the meeting getting underway, it is customary for everyone present to introduce themselves, their role on the IEP team, and how they are involved with the student.

Procedural Safeguards: Federal law requires that the parents or guardians are offered information about their procedural safeguards at least annually. Many districts ask for a signature certifying the procedural safeguards have been received.

Strengths and Concerns: The team discusses the student's strengths and areas of concerns in a broad sense. This is often where the discussion of the necessary related services begins, and this discussion carries into the next sections.

Review Previous Goals: The team reviews progress on the goals from the previous IEP, usually the past year's worth of information. These goals address the skills targeted by the special education and related services provided.

Present Levels of Performance: The IEP team reviews a summary of the student's present levels of academic achievement and functional performance, or PLAAFP. This section contains the information used as the foundation to determine what goals and services are needed. It should include language about how the student's disability affects his or her ability to participate in the general curriculum. The general education classroom teacher would be expected to report about progress in their classroom.

Statement of Proposed Goals: Proposed goals and objectives for the new IEP cycle are discussed. Goals typically involve either academic or functional skills, and are based on the information provided in the PLAAFP. This also is where goals connected to the needed related services are discussed.

Services (Time, Frequency, Duration): The team discusses which special education and related services are needed—including how much time, how often, and for how long—to support the student in addressing their IEP goals. It is important for the general education teacher to be a part of this discussion and help clarify the amount of time a student needs assistance.

State and District Assessments: The team discusses the accommodations the student needs on the mandated state- and district-level assessments (if any). The general education teacher should speak about expectations for state and district assessments.

Placement: The team discusses where the student will receive the needed special education and related services. This should include a discussion of access to nondisabled peers and consideration of the least restrictive environment (LRE). General education classroom teachers, special educators, and related-service providers should discuss expectations for the amount of time the student receives assistance, as well as the location of the service.

Discussion of the necessary related services should be provided to assist the student in accessing the curriculum or participating in class. While the better practice is to embed the discussion of related services into the entire IEP conversation, there often is a separate place on the IEP documentation form to record this information.

Agreement: In most states, agreement is demonstrated by having the parents sign the IEP at the end of the meeting. This indicates support for the proposed program.

FOUR IMPORTANT IEP POINTS FOR CLASSROOM TEACHERS

A classroom teacher has a vital role in the implementation of a student's IEP. We have covered a lot of information about IEPs, but four very important points are worth addressing again, as they are crucial to the success of the IEP team.

First, the general and special education classroom teachers are very important members of the team. They typically refer the student for testing, and they often work with the student every day and see how the student is progressing in the curriculum and interacting with others. Additionally, the classroom teacher input is needed specifically about the curriculum, use of accommodations and modifications, and participation in state and district assessments. It is also important to have the classroom teacher involved in discussion of any other needs of the student and how they access the curriculum.

Second, because the classroom teacher is a very important member of the team and will likely notice problems before others, the teacher can call for a new IEP meeting to discuss issues at any time. It does not have to be a special education teacher or a principal who makes the request. For example, if the student requires greater assistance to access the curriculum, then it would be important for the team to hear when, how, or what is necessary. Unfortunately, many classroom teachers do not realize this is within their responsibility. They may ask the principal about a meeting but not realize they have the authority to request an IEP meeting. We've said it before, but it bears repeating: Classroom teachers spend a great amount of time with the student and can serve as a first line of defense when it comes to identifying needs or requesting supports. They are crucial members of the IEP team and the collaborative efforts to support the educational needs of students.

Third, it is very important for the classroom teacher to preserve confidentiality with all the information shared about the student. Everyone is legally required to maintain confidentiality and to only talk with others who need to know about the student. This includes all conversations with related-service providers. If the classroom teacher is unsure about the policy for confidentiality in their district, then they should reach out to the IEP case manager or other special education personnel to learn more.

Fourth, a teacher is required to attend the IEP meeting. If possible, all teachers who work with the student should attend the meeting to fully convey thoughts and ideas about the student to others and to understand what is expected of them in the implementation of the IEP. Teachers are still required to implement the IEP even if they do not attend the meeting. This includes understanding the instructional and intervention practices they are expected to provide, the accommodations and modifications they are to implement, the necessary related services provided to the student, and what data reports and progress monitoring they are responsible for to help the student make progress in the curriculum and toward the IEP goals.

SUMMARY

This chapter covers a lot of information about the requirements and considerations for related services. As mentioned at the beginning, we hope that some of this content feels like review for you, while other components may help fill in gaps or answer questions for you and your team. We encourage you to use the following "Questions to Consider" to help with that learning or review process. We also encourage you to explore the resources found at the end of the book, including the case studies and their "Questions to Consider" in Appendix A.

KEY TERMS

better practices: practices that may go beyond what the law requires but allows special educators to meet the legal requirements of developing and implementing special education programs so the student can progress in their unique educational needs.

extended school year (ESY): individualized services to help a child maintain skills and not lose progress toward goals during an extended period when school is not in session, such as summer break.

free appropriate public education (FAPE): the education to which every student is entitled under IDEA. Every student is entitled to an education that is appropriate for their unique needs and provided at no cost to the parents or guardians.

individualized education program (IEP): a legal document between the school district and the parents or guardians that defines special education services for an individual child eligible to receive special education; also individualized education plan.

Individuals with Disabilities Education Act (IDEA): a law that guarantees educational rights to all students with disabilities and makes it illegal for school districts to refuse to educate a student based on their disability.

least restrictive environment (LRE): a mandate in IDEA that students with disabilities should be educated to the maximum extent appropriate with their nondisabled peers.

medical services: services that can only be provided by a licensed physician; exempt from the definition of *related services* unless needed for diagnostic or evaluative purposes.

present levels of academic achievement and functional performance (PLAAFP): a component of an IEP that defines a student's strengths and weaknesses, current levels of academic achievement, and functional performance. The information in the PLAAFP directs the creation of goals and determination of needed special education and related services. Sometimes referred to as *present levels*, *PLEP*, *PLAP*, *PLOP*, and other abbreviated terms used locally in districts and regions.

regulations: instructions written by the executive branch that provide direction on how to implement and enforce laws passed by Congress. Special educators must be aware of federal and state regulations pertaining to special education law.

related services: transportation and such developmental, corrective, and other supportive services as are required to help a child with a disability benefit from special education.

special education: education specially designed to meet the unique needs of a child with a disability.

QUESTIONS TO CONSIDER

1. Where can you find information about your state regulations for special education?
2. What are the two important components of an IEP that enable a student to make progress?
3. Why is it important to view an IEP as a road map for students? How does this idea influence your perspective as an IEP team member?
4. How is the need for related services determined for a student?
5. How can IEP team conversations for eligible students improve when the team members emphasize the concept of a free appropriate public education (FAPE)?
6. For students who require related services, how can their plans improve when the IEP team members emphasize access to special education?
7. When thinking about related services in your building, district, or division, in what environments are students provided special education and related services? How does this connect with what you have read about least restrictive environment (LRE)?

Chapter Three

Types and Examples of Related Services

As described in chapter 1, the term *related services* covers a broad array of supports and services available to students eligible for special education. In early conversations while preparing this book, we wanted what most people would want: a complete list that could be the go-to source for educators who need answers fast. Now, before you judge us, we do know better. We know the very definition of *related services* in the law precludes the possibility of a "complete" list. We know related services are determined for the individual student, not by the disability category. We also know there are more examples of related services than we could reasonably and effectively cover in this book, especially given the individualized nature of the work we do to support students in special education. But we still wanted to create something beneficial to you, the educators who work with students every day.

Our goal here is not to provide an exhaustive list but rather a structure for thinking about related services. You'll notice we strayed from the alphabetical list we use in chapter 1 and moved into five categories. We hope these categories make sense based on the type of student need and the type of related-service support. We know learning happens when connections are made and when we can group things into categories, so we hope this structure is a helpful resource for you. We hope this chapter helps you recognize the expertise of the related-service providers and encourages you to collaborate with them, not only as integral members of the IEP team, but also as valued members of the school community. Our five general categories of the common types of related services come from what we've seen in practice, document reviews, and input from countless professionals who work with students every day. Along with the common types of related services, we offer some examples within each category, information on the qualifications of professionals who are experts in these areas, and credible resources for you to explore to learn more. You can find additional resources in chapter 7. We also encourage you to think about these categories and connect them to the case studies of Max, Saraiah, and Angelus in Appendix A.

COMMUNICATION SERVICES

Communication is a vital component of everyday life. It involves skills that affect your ability to hear, listen, understand, speak, read, and write. Students who need these related services may have cognitive, physical, or emotional difficulties that negatively influence their ability to communicate with the world around them and access the academic and social aspects of school. This communication can occur verbally, visually, and in written form. Common related services in this category include speech-language, audiological, and interpreting services. We briefly explore some of these related services and identify the professionals who provide them.

Speech-Language

Speech-language (Sp-Lg) services are the most common services provided to students with IEPs (US Department of Education, 2021). These services are unique in that they are areas of eligibility for both special education services (speech impairment or sound system disorder and language impairment) and related services (speech and/or language services) within IDEA law. Students who require these services can be eligible for special education in any area, such as learning disabilities, autism, emotional disturbance, or other health impairment. Speech-language services are identified and supervised by speech-language pathologists (SLPs), who are required to receive specialized training through graduate programming and hold national certification of clinical competence (CCC) from the American Speech-Language-Hearing Association (ASHA, 2022). SLPs often provide these services directly but can also supervise others in the implementation of the prescribed services as written in the IEP. Students who require Sp-Lg services need support in the mechanical aspects of speaking (voice, fluency, articulation) and/or the language-based skills of understanding or expressing thoughts and ideas (receptive and expressive language), reading, writing, processing information, and interacting socially. SLPs also offer supports for feeding and swallowing disorders that interfere with safety, well-being, and educational performance (ASHA, 2015). The best resource to access for more information on SLPs is the ASHA website (www.asha.org), which has information specifically for school-based services, as well as resources designed for specific audiences, such as parents and guardians, educators, and clinicians.

Audiological Services

Audiology services include identification of the range, nature, and degree of hearing loss, as well as the services needed for skill development and accessing the educational environment. The professional certification and credentialing for audiologists is also conducted by ASHA, with the highest training resulting in a national certificate of clinical competence in audiology (CCC-A; ASHA, 2002). In many districts, there is not a full-time audiologist on staff. Instead, they offer consultative services and limited amounts of direct service for the student, and they primarily support the educators. Let's be honest: They train teachers. The audiologist or hearing specialist in your district often will come to your school, assess the acoustic environment in the classroom, and suggest how to maximize access. They will teach you how to change hearing aid batteries, use FM systems for amplification, and serve as a resource for you as you identify new challenges throughout the school year. They will rely on you to track progress and provide data that will be used in IEP team decisions about future services. For guidelines for audiology services in and for schools, please see ASHA (2002).

Interpreting Services

Interpreting services are provided for students who need the auditory language of the environment provided in a visual way. The most common example is having a sign language interpreter service for the student. This may involve a number of professionals who interact with the student, as sign language interpreters will trade off during the day because this can be exhausting work. Additionally, other technology-based options for interpretation could be considered by the IEP team. Access to technology has increased significantly with many speech-to-text and text-to-speech options available to support reading and writing skills. The professionals involved with providing interpreter services could include an audiologist, speech-language pathologist, or hearing specialist. Federal regulations address interpreting from the standpoint of auditory access, not from a language-difference perspective; supports for students who speak languages other than English are addressed under the "Special Considerations" section of the IEP. If you want to learn more about interpreting services available in your district, contact your special education administrator.

PHYSICAL SERVICES

Many related services are connected to physical abilities and needs of the student, such as vision, hearing, and motor skills. The student has a need based on a physical difference or structural impact. These services connect to physical differences, disabilities, or impairments, as well as the ability to access educational spaces and content. Common examples of services in this category include orientation and mobility, physical therapy, occupational therapy, and recreational therapy. The following are brief explorations of some related services and the professionals who provide them.

Orientation and Mobility

Orientation and mobility (O&M), involves two main components: (1) orientation, which involves knowing one's position in relation to other objects in one's surroundings and keeping track of how these relations and positions change as one moves through the environment, and (2) mobility, the act of moving from one location to another. O&M works to develop the conceptual understanding of the environment, including physical layout and spatial relationships among people, places, and things, and is the foundation for orientation. For more information, please see the resources available from the National Federation for the Blind (2023).

Physical Therapy

Physical therapy services address posture, muscular strength, mobility, and organization of movements in educational environments. These services are identified and supervised by a physical therapist (PT) and can be implemented by a physical therapy assistant (PTA), with both required to receive specialized training (American Physical Therapy Association, 2022b). In many districts, there is not a full-time PT/PTA on staff. These professionals offer consultative services and limited amounts of direct service for the student, but they can teach you how to incorporate therapy skills into the classroom to support generalization. They may rely on you to track progress and provide data to be used in IEP team decisions about future services. For more information about PT/PTA services in and for schools, please see American Physical Therapy Association (APTA, 2022a).

Occupational Therapy

Occupational therapy services include improving, developing, or restoring functions, as well as performing tasks and accessing the educational environment. These services are identified and supervised by an occupational therapist (OT) and can be implemented by an occupational therapy assistant (OTA), who are required to receive specialized training (American Occupational Therapy Association, 2022). In many districts, there is not a full-time OT/OTA on staff. They offer consultative services and limited amounts of direct service for the student, but they will teach you how to incorporate therapy skills into the classroom to support generalization. They may rely on you to track progress and provide data to be used in IEP team decisions about future services. For more information about OT/OTA services in and for schools, please see American Occupational Therapy Association (AOTA, 2023).

Recreational Therapy

Recreational therapy, also known as therapeutic recreation, is a systematic process that uses recreation and other activity-based interventions to address the assessed needs of individuals with illnesses and disabling conditions to improve psychological and physical health, recovery, and well-being. For more information about the service and the credentialing of professionals who provide this service, please see the National Council for Therapeutic Recreation Certification (2023).

SOCIAL, EMOTIONAL, AND PSYCHOLOGICAL SERVICES

A third category of related services involves supports for social, emotional, and mental health knowledge, skills, and growth. These services support students in their ability to access the special education services they need, along with the general education curriculum. Examples of services in this category include psychological, counseling, social work, and parent counseling and training. We briefly explore some of these related services and identify the professionals who provide them.

Psychological Services

Psychologists are available to enhance the educational performance of students by addressing issues related to learning, emotional well-being, and social competence. This goal is accomplished through psychological evaluation for special education and intervention when appropriate, multidisciplinary team problem solving in the response-to-intervention (RtI) process through the early-intervention team (EIT), short-term counseling, collaboration with the mental health community, and consultation with staff. These services are delivered to help eligible children with disabilities benefit from their special education. They may be provided by a school psychologist, school counselors, or school social workers. While not all schools have a full-time school psychologist or social worker on staff, most have a school counselor. For this reason, we focus this section on that professional role. School counselor responsibilities may include but are not limited to

- offering curriculum guidance lessons and individual and group counseling sessions that are culturally responsive and inclusive of the accommodations provided to students with special needs;
- providing short-term, goal-focused counseling in instances where it is appropriate to include these strategies as a part of the IEP or 504 plan;
- encouraging family involvement in the educational process;
- consulting and collaborating with staff and families to understand the special needs of a student and understanding the accommodations and modifications needed to assist the student;
- advocating for students with special needs in the school and in the community;
- contributing to the school's multidisciplinary team within the scope and practice of the school counseling program;
- identifying students who may need to be assessed to determine special education (IEP) or 504 plan eligibility;
- collaborating with other related student support professionals (e.g., school psychologists, physical therapists, occupational therapists, special education staff, speech-language pathologists) in the delivery of services; and
- providing assistance with developing academic, transition, and postsecondary plans for students with IEPs and 504 plans as appropriate counseling services, including rehabilitation counseling.

It is clear from this list that the school counselor is an important related-service provider and should be an integral part of the school community and IEP team. For more information, please see American School Counselor Association (2022).

Social Work Services in Schools

This is an area of increasing need. There are many parts of a student's program that a social worker may assist with, including

- participating in special education assessment meetings and IEP meetings;
- working with those problems in a child's living situation that affect the child's adjustment in school (i.e., home, school, and community);

- preparing a social or developmental history on a child with a disability;
- counseling (group, individual, and/or family);
- mobilizing family, school, and community resources to enable the child to learn as effectively as possible in his or her educational program; and
- assisting in developing positive behavioral intervention strategies.

With the problems many students experienced during the COVID-19 pandemic, it is important to address the other needs of the student. This can often be done with the assistance of a social worker. For more information on the professional training and specific roles of a school social worker, please see School Social Work Association of America (n.d.).

PARENT COUNSELING AND TRAINING

The purpose of parent counseling and training is to assist parents in acquiring skills to support the implementation of their child's Individualized Education Program (IEP). In some cases, this may involve helping the parent to gain skills needed to support IEP goals and objectives at home [Individuals with Disabilities Education Act, 2006, 34 CFR 300.34 (a)]. This is accomplished by

- assisting parents in understanding the educational needs of their child;
- providing parents with information about child development;
- providing support and basic information about a child's initial placement in special education; and
- providing parents with contact information about parent support groups, financial assistance resources, and other potential sources of information or support outside the school system.

Often, parent counseling is provided by the school psychologist. For more information on this role, please see a wonderful resource from the National Association of School Psychologists (NASP, 2021).

MEDICAL AND HEALTH SERVICES

The fourth category is centered on medical and health needs. In chapter 2, we discussed the legal distinction between medical services and what schools are responsible for providing. The bright-line test reminds us that medical services that can only be provided by a physician and are required for diagnostic or evaluative purposes are considered related services. Additionally, medically based services that can be delivered by a nonphysician also can be considered related services and must be provided by the school district, regardless of financial or staffing burdens (Yell, 2019). We briefly explore some of these related services and identify the professionals who provide them.

School Health Services and School Nurse Services

Typically thought of as what the school nurse can provide, many school teams might not realize these could be related services. The specific roles and responsibilities of health care providers is fairly extensive and unfamiliar to many educators. To support learning in this area, chapter 5, on school health services, includes a questionnaire for IEP teams to determine the appropriate services a student might receive. Licensed practical nurses (LPN) and registered nurses (RN) offer the following:

- First aid for accidents and/or sudden illness
- Storage, dispensation, and accountability for prescribed medications
- Adherence to state mandates for student immunizations and physical exam requirements
- Mandated screening programs for hearing and vision
- Assistance to students who are managing ongoing health issues
- Monitoring and containment of actual or potential communicable illnesses and infestations

Medical Services for Diagnostic or Evaluation Purposes

The related-service definition includes medical services that are "for diagnostic and evaluation purposes only" (Individuals with Disabilities Education Act, 2006, 34 C.F.R. § 300.34). The Supreme Court has made it clear that medical services are beyond the scope of IDEA's related services, but this does not mean that school teams can ignore the medical needs of the students, and the IEP team should be able to address specifically what is necessary for the student to participate in school. This especially includes students who have unmet mental health needs that interfere with academic and interpersonal success. However, monitoring medication typically has been regarded as a medical service that goes beyond diagnosis and evaluation and therefore is excluded from a school's responsibility.

MISCELLANEOUS SPECIAL SERVICES

As with any categorization system, we need a space for other services that don't logically fit within the provided categories. Given the individualized nature of special education, it only makes sense there are some unique related services. We briefly explore two of these here.

Early Identification and Assessment of Disabilities in Children

Early identification for special education is crucial for many students, as it allows for the provision of services prior to the student's typical age of school attendance. Many students eligible under early identification also have other needs associated with their disability and likely require related services. The most common related service for students eligible under early identification is speech-language assistance. For more information on this area, consult with the special education administrators in your district.

Transportation

This is a confusing topic for a lot of educators. Transportation is listed in the "Special Considerations" section of the IEP, but not many educators are familiar with the process for determining if it is needed as a related service. Even more difficult is the depth and extent of access, safety, and procedural considerations that must be addressed, from the basics of a seatbelt or harness to the procedure for transferring possession of a student's AAC device in the transition from home to school and back again. We recognize this can be an uncomfortable conversation. It's likely you were not trained on all the aspects of transportation, but you must address it at every IEP meeting. We devote chapter 4 to transportation and provide you with a checklist of things to consider. We hope this resource is helpful as you consider not only how to develop the transportation plan but also how to execute and monitor the plan to ensure student access and success.

SUMMARY

This chapter offers an overview of the common types of related services in five categories: (1) communication services; (2) physical services; (3) social, emotional, and psychological services; (4) medical and health services; and (5) miscellaneous services. If you're like most educators, some of these related services were likely unfamiliar to you. Hopefully, this chapter encourages you to reach out to the related-service providers in your district and strengthen the collaborative conversations. We hope you'll explore the resources provided as you are learning more about the skills and expertise related-service providers bring to your IEP team and school community. We also hope these categories and resources are helpful to you and your team as you consider the individualized needs of the students with IEPs in your school and district. As you think about the information covered in this chapter, you've likely recognized your perspectives through different lenses: as an individual, as part of a school community, and as part of the IEP team. The following "Questions to Consider" are structured with the same frame.

KEY TERMS

audiologists: specially trained professionals who help prevent, diagnose, and treat hearing and balance disorders for people of all ages.

bright-line test: a clearly stated and easy-to-follow rule.

medical services: services that can only be provided by a licensed physician; exempt from the definition of related services, unless needed for diagnostic or evaluative purposes.

occupational therapy (OT): services to improve, develop, or restore functions of activities required for daily life.

orientation and mobility (O&M): a profession focused on instructing individuals with visual impairments or blindness on safe and effective travel throughout their environments.

physical therapy (PT): service to address posture, muscular strength, mobility, and organization of movements.

recreational therapy (RT): a systematic process that uses recreation and other activity-based interventions to address the assessed needs of individuals with illnesses and/or disabling conditions to improve psychological and physical health, recovery, and well-being.

related services: transportation and such developmental, corrective, and other supportive services required to help a child with a disability benefit from special education.

response to intervention (RtI): a multitiered approach to the early identification and support of students with learning and behavior needs.

speech-language services: services to address deficits in (1) the mechanical aspects of speaking (voice, fluency, articulation); (2) the language-based skills of understanding and expressing thoughts and ideas (receptive and expressive language), reading, writing, processing information, and interacting socially; and (3) feeding and swallowing skill deficits that interfere with safety, well-being, and educational performance.

QUESTIONS TO CONSIDER

Individual

Thinking about the four encompassing categories of related services (communication; physical; social, emotional, and psychological; and medical and health), consider the following:

- With which categories are you most familiar? Within the categories, were there specific related services that were more familiar than others?
- Within those familiar related services, was there any knowledge or skill of the related-service provider that was unfamiliar to you?
- What categories of related services were new to you?

Schoolwide Community

- Who are the current people in the related-service provider roles at your building?
- Now that you are empowered with the knowledge of what a related-service provider does, how will you better use their expertise at your school?
- How do you invite a related-service provider to share their expertise at your school (conversations, grade-level meetings, staff meetings, etc.)?
- How do you invite the related-service providers to learn from the classroom and content experts in your building?

IEP Paperwork, Team, and Process

- How does understanding related-service categories and skills influence how you will craft plans for students?
- What are the procedures in your district and building when you receive an IEP for a student that includes a related service you do not have readily available at your school site?
- What are the processes in your district when you receive an IEP for a student that includes a related service unfamiliar to you?

Chapter Four

Transportation as a Related Service

This chapter explains the components of the transportation assessment and clarifies the use of the form. Similar to the chapter on aide support, this chapter walks through the transportation assessment form, explains questions and why they are important, and provides guidance and additional information that will help an IEP team in determining transportation needs for eligible students with disabilities. It is recommended that IEP teams consider every eligible student's needs for transportation at the minimum on an annual basis or more frequently if there are changes to the students' home, road construction, or behavior problems warranting additional supervision. For students who may need additional supervision or aide support for transportation, please see chapter 5, specifically the section on behavioral supports.

The purpose of this form is fairly straightforward: to assist IEP teams in making appropriate transportation determinations. As noted in other chapters, all decisions about a student need to be made related to the student's individual needs and not based on student's disability label. Do not assume that all students with autism can walk to school, and do not assume that all students with physical disabilities require special or modified transportation. It depends on the *individual* needs of the student.

This is not a crisis plan with contacts in case there is a transportation emergency. There may be additional questions raised not covered by this form, so please add whatever questions or comments are necessary. This form is not intended to provide legal guidance related to transportation, just questions that IEP teams should ask to ensure that students receive the transportation necessary to attend the programs that are provided.

Two other important points: First, the individuals who are provided the information on this form are on a need-to-know basis. Work with the staff on the importance of confidentiality and not disclosing unnecessary information to others. Second, the answers from this form may need to be modified regularly. Work to make sure those who need to know about the changes are given the information so they can provide safe and reliable transportation for the student. A nonannotated copy of the form is included at the end of the chapter.

TRANSPORTATION ASSESSMENT

Meeting date: _____

Student name: _____

Date of birth: _____ Grade level: _____

Disability/disabilities: _____

School attending: _____

District: _____

Case manager: _____

Related services: _____

Level of support: _____

Date of last IEP revision: _____

Meeting Date: Always include the meeting date on the form. There may be updates provided during the year and additional meetings when new information is obtained. For subsequent meetings, either use a new form or make notes off to the side indicating the date and the members of the team who participated.

Student Name, Date of Birth, Grade Level, Disability/Disabilities: The basic student information should also be included in this form and should be the same as the central database the district keeps for the child's attendance.

School Attending, District, Case Manager, Related Services, Level of Support: This may seem straightforward, but as districts are increasingly consolidating services with other districts, it is important to understand the sending district, the case manager for the student, and other basic information about the student.

Other: Information about how to contact the parents or guardians and other important individuals should be included as a part of a crisis plan that would be a part of every student's transportation.

TRANSPORTATION INFORMATION

Address: _____

City: _____ State: _____ Zip: _____

Phone: _____

Guardian name(s): _____

Who can get child off the bus? _____

Guardians' cell phone number(s): _____

Guardians' email address(es): _____

District of residence: _____

Classroom location: _____

District resident? If not, clarify: _____

Length of ride: _____

Address: The address of the student may be different from the pick-up or drop-off location for the student. Make sure this is clear for whomever is providing the transportation.

Guardian Name(s): The guardian's name is included as a point of contact. This would also be included as a part of any crisis plan.

Who can get child off the bus? Some students may have individuals other than the parents who can help the student get off the bus or meet the student. This could be a designated adult, day-care provider, designated neighbor, or relative. Ask this question to determine who will be meeting the student when they leave the bus. More on this in another section.

Guardians' Cell Phone Number(s): Not all parents or guardians have access to the use of their cell phone during school hours, so include the numbers to contact during regular school hours.

Guardians' Email Address: Not all parents use email for communication, so seek the preferred method of communication.

District of Residence: As more students are served as a part of consortium of shared classes, listing the district in which the student resides clarifies responsibilities when there are problems.

Classroom Location: Classroom location clarifies the specific school and possibly even the location of the classroom within the school to facilitate where the student should be dropped off for their education.

District resident? If not, clarify: District residents will have the same answer as the previous "District of Residence."

Length of Ride: This is the typical length of ride for the student. Not the ideal. Not the shortest. Be realistic about the amount of time the student spends on the bus.

CAN THIS STUDENT BE TRANSPORTED WITH THEIR PEERS?

Yes, with no modifications or support

Yes, with modifications (specify): _____

No, they need special transportation with modifications (specify):

_____

Can this student be transported with their peers? The IEP team should have the preference that the student will be transported with their peers to the maximum extent possible. It is very important to make all determinations about whether the student can be transported with their peers based not on the disability label of the student but on the individual needs of the student. Do not assume that all students with physical disabilities will require special transportation. Also, some students who do not have a physical disability may require special transportation assistance.

Some students who live in a close geographical proximity to the school and do not require special transportation to get to and from school may need transportation training. This may involve instruction on road crossings, determining safe routes to and from school, and additional supervision from school personnel. A staff person may need to be assigned to this task.

The determination about special transportation needs should be made annually or more frequently if there are changes to either the student's location of education or residence, road construction, physical needs, weather-related incidents, behavioral needs, or other problems noted by members of the IEP team.

If the student requires modifications in order to access transportation with nondisabled peers, then do whatever possible to make these modifications as unobtrusive as possible and not call attention to the supports the student is receiving. For example, if a student needs an aide for a seizure disorder, ask, "Does the aide need to sit immediately next to the student on the bus, or does the aide just need to be on the bus in case of a seizure?"

> **ROUTE CHANGE CONSIDERATIONS**
>
> - To meet the student's medical or behavioral needs
> - Problems with certain locations that must be avoided
> - Sounds/smells/problems with highways
> - To lessen exposure to traffic
> - Length of time on bus
> - Order of pick-up issues
> - Concern about others on the bus
> - Other: _____

Route Change Considerations: Like an IEP, the transportation plan for the student is not fixed, and changes should be made when necessary. Any member of the IEP team, along with others in the education community, should pay attention to the needs of the students and report to others if there are problems or even if there are perceived problems.

If the student has behavioral needs, there should be regular monitoring of the student, along with data about what works and what does not work. As mentioned earlier, the preference should be to have the student traveling with their nondisabled peers to the maximum extent possible. Keep this in mind when dealing with students' behaviors.

Questions to ask about behavioral needs relate to the safety of the student, as well as the safety of others. The standard question as a part of IEP development should be asked here: Does the student engage in behaviors that affect their transportation and the transportation of others? Think broadly. Pay attention to all the steps related to accessing transportation, and if a student has problems with one or more area, then develop a plan to address the issue. Example steps include waiting for the bus or van, getting on the bus or van, riding the bus or van, and exiting the bus or van.

If the student has medical needs, then make sure the parents work to keep the school staff aware of the student's needs and whether the needs change with medication, temperature, or if there are allergies in different seasons. For example, in some areas of the country, there are students who have severe problems with seasonal pollen, others who have problems with dust, or others who have problems when farms commence spraying to ready for the spring planting. Pay attention to these needs, and be ready to adjust when necessary.

Are there problems with certain locations that must be avoided? This addresses not only the behavioral needs of some students, where a student may have an emotional reaction to a certain location, but also the stimulation of the crowds, noise, or traffic may pose a problem. Some students may have previous experiences related to bullying, and the memories of those incidents may cause problems for the student.

As noted earlier, some students have problems with sounds, smells, or other issues with certain roadways. There are some students who have sensory issues with certain sounds, such as excessive car horns, sirens, or plane sounds, that may pose a problem while they are riding the bus or van. Other students may have severe issues with certain smells, which can include pesticides, factories, exhaust, or chemical plants. Pay attention to the sensory needs of the student, and work to address this when needed and whenever possible. Finally, pay attention to whether the student has problems either behaviorally or emotionally to riding on the highway. This form addresses the length of the ride later, but other factors make highway riding difficult for some students.

WEATHER FACTORS

Clarify: _____

Protocol: _____

STREET/SIDEWALK CONDITIONS

Clarify: _____

Protocol: _____

Weather Factors: Some students' transportation plans will need to be modified due to weather factors. These factors can include snow, ice, rain, and wind. Some routes students travel may be affected by severe weather, and we must plan ahead of time. Questions to ask in this section include, "Can the wheelchair/walker/crutches make it through the snow/ice to safely get on and off the school bus?" "Does extreme cold or heat affect the student while they are either waiting for or riding the bus?" "For students who walk to school or those who walk to the bus, do the weather conditions allow them to make this trip safely?"

> **PICK-UP AND DROP-OFF NOTES**
>
> - Pull in drive to pick up and drop off
> - Pick up and drop off on residence side
> - Pick up requires medicine or device from parents or guardians (specify): _____
>
> - Pick up and drop off at school entrance allows for less congestion or more supervision
> - Supervision required when dropped off at school (specify): _____
> _____
>
> - Other: _____

Pick-Up and Drop-Off Notes: Where to drop off the student is very important, as some students need to be dropped off on a certain side of the road, while others need the van or bus to pull into the student's driveway to drop off the student.

Pick up requires medicine or device from parents or guardians: Is there medication that needs to be picked up from or delivered back to the parents or guardians? Is there a medical device or other equipment that needs to be picked up from or delivered back to the parents or guardians? Who will make this handoff? What is the protocol when the parents or guardians are not there? How is the medication stored while on the bus? Who is the point of contact with the bus supervisor?

Pick up and drop off at school entrance allows for less congestion or more supervision: The policy should be to include the students to the maximum extent possible, which includes not unnecessarily segregating the student. However, there may be a need to have the student be dropped off at school at a different location that either provides less congestion or, due to behavior, more supervision. This decision about changing where the student is dropped off should be made based on the student's needs, not on the disability label.

Supervision required when dropped off at school: Does the student require supervision when they are dropped off either at school or at home? If the student requires supervision at school, who is assigned to meet the student and bring them into school? If the student requires supervision when they are dropped off at home, who will meet the student? Is there a secondary contact if that person is not there?

Other: Other points that could be addressed include different people for different days or the medical device only comes home on weekends and longer holidays. How should changes to the pick-up and drop-off schedule be documented?

SEATING ON BUS OR VAN

- Front of bus or van
- Back of bus or van
- Assigned seat
- Seating with limited access to other riders
- Away from door or window
- Window seat
- Seated with feet on floor or low-floor bus
- Seated out of emergency exits
- Seated with seat belt on
- Seated with harness only
- Seated with seat belt and harness
- Seated with car seat or booster seat
- Seated next to aide
- Other devices necessary for travel: _____
- Other: _____

Seating on Bus or Van: The seating of the student on the bus or van should be considered before the completion of this questionnaire. Is the student to sit at the front? Does the student, due to behaviors, need to sit in a seat away from the driver? The needs and behaviors of other students are to be considered in this section. Are there other students on the bus or van where there needs to be a clear separation? Are there locations on the bus or van that need to be considered? Are there windows on the bus that the student needs to be separated from? Does the student need to be seated away from or near an emergency row? Does the student need a seat belt, harness, or both? If the answer is yes, then who is responsible for ensuring the seat belt or harness is attached? Who is responsible for putting the child into the seat belt or harness, and who is responsible for removing the child?

Does the student need to be seated next to an aide? If so, is the aide a behavioral aide or a medical aide? See the aide forms in chapter 5. Can the aide just be on the bus, or does the aide need to sit next to the student? What is the protocol if the aide is absent and cannot ride the bus or van?

Other devices necessary for travel: Are other devices or calming tools necessary for the student to ride the van/bus? If so, where will they be stored, and who is responsible for ensuring they are on van or bus?

Other: This is the space to make notes of any other pertinent considerations for the bus or van ride. Maybe the family members have special tips or suggestions to ensure a safe and efficient ride for the student.

BEHAVIORS

- Does the student have behavior problems on the bus?
  Yes (specify): _____

  No

- Who should the bus driver contact if there is a behavior issue?
  _____

- Add any relevant behaviors from the BIP: _____

Does the student have behavior problems on the bus? As covered in another chapter, each IEP team asks, "Does the student exhibit behaviors that impede their learning or that of others?" When asked about classroom environments, the team is expected to develop a positive behavior support plan based on a functional assessment of behavior and using positive behavior techniques. The same is true in thinking about transportation. Just because a student has behavior problems does not mean they should be automatically removed from the bus or van.

Results of the functional assessment of behavior should be listed in the "Present Levels" section of the IEP, with a clear, measurable plan to address the behavior in the "Goals" and "Specially Designed Instruction" sections of the IEP.

Details about the behaviors should be noted, along with steps taken to improve the behaviors. Periodically suspending the student is not a behavior-management strategy that provides instruction to the student about appropriate behavior. For some students, this strategy may reinforce behaviors because the student may receive more, different, or separate attention that they are seeking.

Finally, when the student does engage in a behavior that causes problems, there should be clear steps about how the behavior should be documented and to whom the behavior should be reported. As much as possible, the reporting of the behavior should include what was happening immediately prior to the occurrence of the behavior and what happened immediately after the behavior. The description, if possible, should also include whether this behavior has occurred before and what steps or strategies have been tried before.

DISCHARGE OF STUDENT

Can this student be discharged from the bus or van without an adult waiting to receive them?

Yes

No

If no adult is present, who should be called? _____

_____

Can this student be discharged from the bus or van without an adult waiting to receive them? As has been covered elsewhere on this form, the team should ask about the supervision of the student when they are dropped off. This applies to when they are being dropped off not only at home but also at school. If there is no adult present, who should be called? This number should also be a part of any crisis or emergency plan that a district would create for a student as a part of any form of transportation.

SUPERVISION/ASSISTANCE WHEN TAKING TRANSPORTATION

- To board bus and on steps
- To remain safe in "danger zone" from all sides of the bus
- To cross street or safely navigate into home and school
- To stay seated upright on the seat in the compartment
- To maintain appropriate and safe behavior
- To avoid contact with emergency exits
- To avoid putting anything out the windows
- To navigate emergency exits
- To leave bus in the event of an emergency:

    Person(s) responsible: _____

    Level of assistance: _____

Supervision/Assistance When Taking Transportation: This section goes into greater detail about the supervision necessary when waiting for and riding the bus. As a part of transportation training, we need to make sure the student has received instruction based on their needs, but it typically involves the four steps of bus riding: (1) waiting for the bus, (2) getting on the bus, (3) riding the bus, and (4) getting off the bus. The questions in this section address these areas and walk through potential problems before they occur. Some of the questions may be duplicative of other sections but are addressed here to deal with the training necessary for the safety of the student.

Does the student need supervision in getting on the bus? Is the supervision necessary due to a behavioral issue, or is the supervision due to a physical issue? Does the student require assistance navigating the door and the possible steps to get on the bus or van?

Does the student need supervision to prevent them from going in front of the bus, behind the bus, or into any areas that may be out of sight of the bus driver or an oncoming vehicle? Does the student need assistance in crossing the street after they disembark from the bus or van? What side of the street should the bus or van drop off the student?

Does the student need supervision to remain safely seated? The student may need a seatbelt or harness or may require an aide to remind them of what they are supposed to be doing on the bus or van.

Does the student have behavior needs requiring an aide? See the earlier behavior questions in addition to the questions about an aide in chapter 5.

Pay attention to potential problems with windows and emergency exits the student may have. Is the student likely to throw something out the window, or could the student trigger the emergency exit latch—even by mistake? Pay attention to where the student may be seated on the van or bus.

If the student needs assistance in navigating emergency exits, how will this be accomplished? Will there be training? Will there be support for the student? What is the protocol for using the emergency exit instead of the regular exit? Who will do the training?

What is the level of assistance the student requires to leave the bus? Who will be trained in providing this assistance? What is the back-up plan if this person is not on the bus or van?

COMMUNICATION

- Verbal
- ESL
- Sign language
- Will communication board be on the bus?

   Yes

   No

- Picture Exchange System
- Gestures
- Other: _____

Communication: Some students will need communication assistance. The questions in this section clarify the specifics of the needs of the student and are fairly self-explanatory. The team should clarify how the student communicates and ensure there is training for the staff working with the student on the bus. The team should also clarify the use of the communication board and how the board will be delivered to the parents and to the staff at the school. Like other sections of this form, this part may need to be modified as the needs and expressive ability of the student changes over time.

EQUIPMENT

- Auditory equipment
- Special items for the student
  Special book
  Transitional item
  Access to music
  Screen device
- Step-stool access
- Safety vest or harness (can be used on traditional bus seat without lap belt or reinforced seat with lap belt)

   Waist size with outer clothing: _____

   Waist size without outer clothing: _____

   Person(s) responsible for putting vest on and off: _____

   Person(s) responsible for connecting vest to mount and taking vest off mount: _____

> Person(s) responsible for installing mount: _____
> - Child safety seat
>   Weight: _____
>   Height: _____
> - Wheelchair
>   Person responsible for attaching chair: _____
> - Safety items on bus
>   Transport auxiliary equipment according to appropriate guidelines
>   Child-safe belt cutter
>   Nonlatex gloves
>   Evacuation blanket
>   Individual student bag
>   Basic first aid kit
>   Emergency numbers
>   Belt extender
>   Body fluid cleanup kit
>   Process and procedure to carry oxygen: _____
>   Other: _____

Equipment: There may be additional or supplemental equipment not listed elsewhere on this form. However, use the list to determine if equipment is necessary and who has the responsibility for ensuring it is provided for the student. This section should include the positions of the people who will have the responsibility of attaching harnesses, attaching wheelchairs, and ensuring the safety items on the bus or van. These safety items are not a comprehensive list. There may be others. Ensure the bus or van is checked regularly to ensure the safety items are on the bus or van, in good working order, and are easily accessible.

It should go without saying, many items on this list require training for the staff on the van or bus. Make sure that when there are changes to the student's protocol, the staff on the van or bus are made aware of the necessary changes and are provided appropriate training.

Transportation of oxygen is potentially dangerous. Ensure the staff have received training on how to transfer, monitor, and use effectively. Also, ensure the staff have training for the use of oxygen and how to monitor it when a student needs support. Finally, ensure the bus is equipped to carry oxygen.

The measurements used for the belt and seat may change as the student grows and changes over time. Periodically make sure the measurements are appropriate for the student and that the straps to secure the student do not cut off blood flow or cause the student to be uncomfortable. Designate a staff person to be responsible for determining on a regular basis if changes are necessary.

Procedural Safeguards for Medical and Behavior Concerns: There may be additional or supplemental information not on this form. Always

---

PROCEDURAL SAFEGUARDS FOR MEDICAL AND BEHAVIOR CONCERNS

- Medical crisis intervention plan (attached)
- Behavioral intervention plan (attached) with training
- Crisis management plan that can be implemented from the bus
- Do-not-resuscitate order

   Person responsible: _____

   Protocol: _____

- Oxygen or ventilator (specify): _____

   Person responsible: _____

   Protocol: _____

- Cardiac problems (specify): _____

   Person responsible: _____

   Protocol: _____

- Seizure precautions (specify): _____

   Person responsible: _____

   Protocol: _____

- Asthma or other respiratory conditions (specify): _____

   Person responsible: _____

   Protocol: _____

- Allergies (specify): _____

- Shunt precautions (specify): _____

  Person responsible: _____

  Protocol: _____

- Feeding tube or significant swallowing problems (specify): _____

  _____

  Person responsible: _____

  Protocol: _____

- Fragile bones or other orthopedic precautions (specify): _____

  _____

- Medication side effects (specify): _____
- Other: _____

ask if there is something else not covered here that needs to be addressed. If there is a medical, behavioral, or crisis plan, then make sure not only that it is attached but also that the staff responsible for the implementation of the plan are fully aware of their responsibilities and that they have their questions about what should be done and when addressed.

Do not take a do-not-resuscitate order lightly. Meet with the family and your general counsel, and seek outside medical counsel regarding this step. Obtain clarity from them before addressing the plan.

For all medical issues, ensure there is appropriate medical training on each issue for the staff. Address the specific needs of the student, making sure the training is provided by individuals who are knowledgeable and certified appropriately for what they do. Provide periodic refresher instruction for the necessary staff.

For each area listed in this section, make sure the staff understands the warning signs, first steps, whom to call, where the necessary equipment is located, and who has responsibility for the implementation of the plan. Each of these areas will likely need to be updated regularly. Keep *all* informed about updates.

Does the student need a test ride? Do not assume the student (and the staff) understand what is necessary for a safe and successful van or bus ride.

TRAINING AND SUPPORT

Does the student need a test ride?

Yes, and date to be completed: _____

No

If the student needs to have their wheelchair strapped into the bus or van, then practice before the first ride is very important. Practice where the equipment will be stored, how it will be handed off to the parents or guardians, and what the protocol is when the van or bus needs to the replaced. Do not assume the information, equipment, and plans will be in place with a new van or bus.

After the practice, meet with the responsible staff to determine if any additional questions need to be addressed and whether the transportation plan needs to be modified.

OTHER

- Will the sending district provide equipment for field trips?

    Yes (specify equipment): _____

    No

- Who is responsible for maintaining and cleaning equipment? _____
  _____

- If the sending district has a weather-related delay, who is responsible for calling

    parents? _____

    bus driver? _____

- If the school district where the classroom is located has a delay, who is responsible for calling

    parents? _____

    bus driver? _____

- If seating needs to be adjusted, who is responsible? _____
  _____

Other: This set of questions relates directly to students who receive their services as a part of a consortium or shared classes with other districts. This is common especially with smaller school districts and with students with more severe disabilities, where districts combine services for low-incidence disabilities. These questions address the responsibility of the sending district and who has responsibility for ensuring the necessary equipment is provided and maintained. These questions also address the necessity for coordinated efforts related to weather delays and ensuring there is a plan prior to any event.

SUMMARY OF TRANSPORTATION PLAN

Date provided to transportation: _____

Date Provided to Transportation: This date should clarify when the plan is provided to the transportation personnel. Just providing the plan to transportation personnel is not enough; make sure questions are addressed and there is an understanding of responsibilities.

NEXT STEPS REQUIRED

Is training required for staff, drivers, parents or guardians, and caregivers?

Yes
- Type of training: _____
- Participants: _____
- Date of training: _____

No

Step to be Taken:	Responsible Party:

Is training required for staff, drivers, parents or guardians, and caregivers? The important part of this section is to highlight the necessary steps to be taken and the responsible party for ensuring the steps occur. Delineate what to do and who should take responsibility for the action. Clarify the specific training necessary for the staff, the bus or van drivers, and any staff who may be also riding on the bus. In the event of a change of personnel, ensure the new personnel are aware of their responsibilities and receive adequate training.

Is transportation training for the student necessary?

Yes (specify): _____

No

Is transportation training for the student necessary? If the student needs transportation training, then ensure the staff who will be working with the student are also aware of the needs and any concerns the student and the family may have about the transportation service. Provide the training early enough so that the plan can be modified, and determine if additional training is necessary for either the student or the staff.

NOTIFICATION TO PARENT OR GUARDIAN

If there are any changes in your child's medical or behavioral status that you believe may affect transportation, please contact one of the following people to assist with the plan:

_____
_____
_____
_____

Notification to Parent or Guardian: This is a very important section. The parents need to know whom to contact if there are any changes or if there are any problems with the plan that need to be addressed. The changes can be due to medical, behavioral, or situational factors that will alter the method or manner in which transportation is provided to the student. The point of contact should then alert the necessary individuals of the changes and consider meeting with the team.

IEP TEAM PARTICIPANTS

Parent/Guardian	Title	Date
Transportation personnel	Title	Date
Team member	Title	Date
Team member	Title	Date

SUMMARY

This chapter provides a frame for the IEP team to consider the transportation needs of an individual student. The transportation assessment form is explained, with comments within each section. The nonannotated copy of the transition assessment is provided at the end of this chapter. As you consider transportation as a related service, we hope these questions are helpful for your thinking, procedures, and processes.

KEY TERMS

aide: a person assigned to assist or support. In special education, an aide can be listed as a service or support on the IEP, with the person assigned to assist or support a student with a particular task or function in order for the student to access special education services. Examples include a health care aide, transportation aide, and so on. Also paraprofessional, parapro, and classroom attendant.

autism: a developmental disability significantly affecting verbal and nonverbal communication and social interaction, usually evident before age 3, that adversely affects a child's educational performance.

harness: a form of protective equipment designed to safeguard a person during transit, such as on a school bus. The harness fits around a person's legs, over their arms, and around their torso.

QUESTIONS TO CONSIDER

1. What does your district or division currently offer for supports when developing plans for transportation? How can you use the resource in this chapter in conjunction with those existing supports?
2. What considerations for the transition assessment were new to you in considering transportation as a related service?
3. How will information for a student's transportation plan be shared with individuals working with the student? How will confidentiality be ensured?
4. What are the procedures for staff to ask questions and collaborate with transportation services?

IEP TRANSPORTATION ASSESSMENT

Meeting date: _____

Student name: _____

Date of birth: _____ Grade Level: _____

Disability/disabilities: _____

School attending: _____

District: _____

Case manager: _____

Related services: _____

Level of support: _____

Date of last IEP revision: _____

TRANSPORTATION INFORMATION

Address: _____

City: _____ State: _____ Zip: _____

Phone: _____

Guardian name(s): _____

Who can get child off the bus? _____

Guardians' cell phone number(s): _____

Guardians' email address(es): _____

District of residence: _____

Classroom location: _____

District resident? If not, clarify: _____

Length of ride: _____

CAN THIS STUDENT BE TRANSPORTED WITH THEIR PEERS?

Yes, with no modifications or support

Yes, with modifications (specify): _____

No, they need special transportation with modifications (specify): ____

_____

ROUTE CHANGE CONSIDERATIONS

- To meet the student's medical or behavioral needs
- Problems with certain locations that must be avoided
- Sounds/smells/problems with highways?
- To lessen exposure to traffic
- Length of time on bus
- Order of pick-up issues
- Concern about others on the bus

- Other: _____

WEATHER FACTORS

Clarify: _____

Protocol: _____

STREET/SIDEWALK CONDITIONS

Clarify: _____

Protocol: _____

PICK-UP AND DROP-OFF NOTES

- Pull in drive to pick up and drop off
- Pick up and drop off on residence side
- Pick up required medicine or device from parents or guardians (specify): _____

- Pick up and drop off at school entrance allows for less congestion or more supervision

- Supervision required when dropped off at school (specify): _____
_____

- Other: _____

SEATING ON BUS OR VAN

- Front of bus or van
- Back of bus or van
- Assigned seat
- Seating with limited access to other riders
- Away from door or window
- Window seat
- Seated with feet on floor or low-floor bus
- Seated out of emergency exits
- Seated with seat belt on
- Seated with harness only
- Seated with seat belt and harness
- Seated with car seat or booster seat
- Seated next to aide

- Other devices necessary for travel: _____
- Other: _____

BEHAVIORS

- Does the student have behavior problems on the bus?

  Yes (specify): _____

  No

- Who should the bus driver contact if there is a behavior issue? ____

  _____

- Add any relevant behaviors from the BIP: _____

DISCHARGE OF STUDENT

Can this student be discharged from the bus or van without an adult waiting to receive them?

Yes

No

If no adult is present, who should be called? _____

SUPERVISION/ASSISTANCE WHEN TAKING TRANSPORTATION

- To board bus and on steps
- To remain safe in "danger zone" from all sides of the bus
- To cross street or safely navigate into home and school
- To stay seated upright on the seat in the compartment
- To maintain appropriate and safe behavior
- To avoid contact with emergency exits
- To avoid putting anything out the windows
- To navigate emergency exits
- To leave bus in the event of an emergency:

  Person(s) responsible: _____

  Level of assistance: _____

COMMUNICATION

- Verbal
- ESL
- Sign language
- Will communication board be on the bus?

  Yes

  No

- Picture Exchange System
- Gestures
- Other: _____

EQUIPMENT

- Auditory equipment
- Special items for the student
  special book
  transitional item
  access to music
  screen device
- Step-stool access
- Safety vest or harness (can be used on traditional bus seat without lap belt or reinforced seat with lap belt)

  Waist size with outer clothing: _____

  Waist size without outer clothing: _____

  Person(s) responsible for putting vest on and off: _____

  Person(s) responsible for connecting vest to mount and taking vest off mount: _____

  Person(s) responsible for installing mount: _____

- Child safety seat

  Weight: _____

  Height: _____

- Wheelchair

  Person responsible for attaching chair: _____

- Safety items on bus
  Transport of auxiliary equipment according to appropriate guidelines
  Child-safe belt cutter
  Nonlatex gloves
  Evacuation blanket
  Individual student bag
  Basic first aid kit
  Emergency numbers
  Belt extender
  Body fluid clean-up kit
  Process and procedure to carry oxygen: _____

  Other: _____

PROCEDURAL SAFEGUARDS FOR MEDICAL AND BEHAVIOR CONCERNS

- Medical crisis intervention plan (attached)
- Behavioral intervention plan (attached) with training
- Crisis management plan that can be implemented from the bus
- Do-not-resuscitate order

  Person responsible: _____

  Protocol: _____

- Oxygen or ventilator (specify): _____

  Person responsible: _____

  Protocol: _____

- Cardiac problems (specify): _____

  Person responsible: _____

  Protocol: _____

- Seizure precautions (specify): _____

  Person responsible: _____

  Protocol: _____

- Asthma or other respiratory conditions (specify): _____

  Person responsible: _____

  Protocol: _____

- Allergies (specify): _____
- Shunt precautions (specify): _____
  Person responsible: _____
  Protocol: _____
- Feeding tube or significant swallowing problems (specify): _____
  Person responsible: _____
  Protocol: _____
- Fragile bones or other orthopedic precautions (specify): _____
  _____
- Medication side effects (specify): _____
- Other: _____

TRAINING AND SUPPORT

Does the student need a test ride?
  Yes, and date to be completed: _____
  No

OTHER

- Will the sending district provide equipment for field trips?
  Yes (specify equipment): _____
  No
- Who is responsible for maintaining and cleaning equipment? _____
  _____
- If the sending district has a weather-related delay, who is responsible for calling
  parents? _____
  bus driver? _____

- If the school district where the classroom is located has a delay, who is responsible for calling

  parents? _____

  bus driver? _____
- If seating needs to be adjusted who is responsible? _____

SUMMARY OF TRANSPORTATION PLAN

Date provided to transportation: _____

NEXT STEPS REQUIRED

Is training required for staff, drivers, parents or guardians, and caregivers?

Yes

- Type of training: _____
- Participants: _____
- Date of training: _____

No

Step to be Taken:	Responsible Party:

Is transportation training for student necessary?

Yes (specify): _____

No

NOTIFICATION TO PARENT OR GUARDIAN

If there are any changes in your child's medical or behavioral status that you believe may affect transportation, please contact one of the following people to assist with the plan:

_____

_____

_____

IEP TEAM PARTICIPANTS

Parent/Guardian	Title	Date
Transportation personnel	Title	Date
Team member	Title	Date
Team member	Title	Date

Chapter Five

Health Care Supports as a Related Service

with Kristin C. Wikel

Many students who have been identified as eligible for special education and related services may also have medical or health needs that must be addressed through health plans. It is very important that schools understand the unique medical needs of their students and enact plans to keep the students safe in the education setting.

This chapter explains the components of a health assessment and clarifies the use of the form. Similar to chapter 4, this chapter walks through the health-level assessment form, explains questions and why they are important, and provides guidance and additional information to help an IEP team determine health support needs for eligible students with disabilities. It is recommended that IEP teams consider whether a student requires assistance for health needs at the minimum annually or more frequently if there are changes to the student's health status or if there are problems warranting additional supervision. For students who may need additional supervision or aide support for transportation due to their health needs, please see chapter 4, specifically the section on health care supports.

The purpose of this form is fairly straightforward: to assist IEP teams in making appropriate health support determinations. As noted in other chapters, all decisions about a student must be made for the student's individual needs and not based on student's disability label. Do not assume that all students with cerebral palsy need health assistance, and do not assume that all students with physical disabilities require special or modified health care support. It depends on the *individual* needs of the student.

This is not a crisis plan with contacts in case there is a health care emergency. There may be additional questions raised not covered by this form; please add whatever questions or comments are necessary. This form is not intended to provide legal guidance on health care needs; it is just questions

IEP teams should ask to ensure students receive the supports necessary to attend the programs that are provided.

Two other important points: First, the individuals who are provided the information on this form are on a need-to-know basis. Work with the staff on the importance of confidentiality and not disclosing unnecessary information to others. Second, the answers from this form may need to be modified regularly. Work to ensure those who need to know about the changes are provided the information so they can provide a safe education for the student. A nonannotated copy of the form is included at the end of the chapter.

MEDICAL AND HEALTH SUPPORTS

Date of meeting: _____

Name: _____

Age: _____

School: _____

Grade level: _____

Disability/disabilities: _____

Primary support: _____

Level of support: _____

Related services: _____

Date of last IEP revision: _____

School attendance:

- Regular school attendance
- Irregular school attendance (explain): _____
  _____
- Seasonal school attendance (explain): _____
  _____

Guardians' cell phone number(s): _____

Guardians' email address(es): _____

Always include the meeting date on the form. There may be updates provided during the year and additional meetings when new information is obtained. For subsequent meetings, either use a new form, or make notes off to the side indicating the date and the members of the team who participated.

The basic student information should also be included in this form and should be the same as the central database the district keeps regarding the child's attendance.

The question about districts may seem straightforward, but as districts are increasingly consolidating services with other districts, it is important to understand the sending district, the case manager for the student, and other basic information about the student.

Include special education eligibility (i.e., disability and/or medical diagnosis) information on the form. Although special education and related services are individualized to the student, it is always beneficial to have the student's disability and health needs identified on the form.

Include information regarding the student's primary level of support while at school, which may include the student's least restrictive environment, nursing care support, and physical needs. Indicate if the student needs assistance with mobility, including assistance in the restroom and activities of daily living. Depending on the student's health needs, the student may require medications and other nursing support throughout the school day. Consider all aspects of the student's day, and detail the type of support the student needs while at school.

Consider each aspect of the student's primary level of support, and indicate what type of support is needed for the student to complete the activity. For example, some students may be dependent for transferring on and off the toilet in the restroom, but the student is independent with clothing management. Other students may be able to eat and drink independently, but some require all liquids to be thickened in order to safely swallow.

Indicate the types of related services that are provided to the students through their IEPs. Having related-service personnel (e.g., occupational therapists, physical therapists, speech-language pathologists) participate in completing this health assessment can be helpful in addressing mobility, fine motor, and communication needs. Also, school nurses should participate in any health assessment needs of students and can address the different types of health supports for students.

Always include the date of the student's last IEP revision on this document. Some students may have new medical needs and could benefit from additional support, goals, or related services provided through the student's IEP. Consider reconvening a case conference to address any new medical needs, including school attendance, in the student's IEP.

Students with chronic health conditions or medical needs may be frequently absent from school. Some students who are frequently absent from school may benefit from supplemental instruction to help them stay caught up with their assignments. Other students may miss school due to seasonal changes in the weather (e.g., severe allergies or respiratory conditions). School personnel may need to obtain releases of information from the student's legal guardians to speak to the student's medical providers regarding school attendance. It may be beneficial for medical providers to write physician statements detailing the impact the student's medical condition has on school attendance. School personnel may need to address how the student will keep up with missed work through the student's IEP.

Information about how to contact the parents and other important individuals should be included as a part of a crisis plan that would be a part of every student's health care plan.

HEALTH SUPPORT

The student *needs* this type of aide, in accordance with a health services plan, to (check all that apply in the school setting):

- Monitor for seizure activity, vital signs, other medical symptoms, or drug side effects. Describe the nature of the activity or symptom for which monitoring is required and, if possible, the actual or expected frequency of such activity or symptoms: _____

  _____

- Medications administered at school: _____
- Implement emergency medical procedures pending arrival of nurse.
- Monitor or make routine adjustments to equipment. Describe the equipment in question: _____
- Assist with toileting or self-care.
- Assist with feeding.
- Nutrition/diet restrictions: _____
- Assist with mobility (wheelchair, walker, lift, positioning, etc.).
- Assist with fine motor (opening containers, writing, typing, etc.).
- Other (describe): _____

It is very important to be detailed in describing the type of medical activity or symptom that should be monitored. In some instances, it may be beneficial for the student's medical provider to describe symptoms of the student's medical condition and possible adverse medical side effects. You may need to obtain releases from the student's legal guardians to speak to the student's medical provider(s).

Discuss with the student's legal guardians the types of medications that will be administered during the school day. Include any emergency-type medications (e.g., rescue inhalers, emergency seizure medications) in this section, as well. Review the school district's policy for dispensing medication with the student's legal guardians.

Review the school district's emergency medical procedures with the student's legal guardians, and attach a copy of the protocols to this document. Emergency procedures that are specific to the student, such as a seizure action plan for students with epilepsy, should be detailed in the student's health plan.

Describe in detail the type of medical equipment that the student will be bringing to school. Be specific in describing the types of adjustments that may be made on the student's medical equipment. Discuss how and when the student's legal guardians will be notified if an adjustment is made on the student's medical equipment. In some instances, medical equipment may alarm in the event of a medical emergency, and emergency medical procedures may be needed. Specific training may be needed for school staff to adjust and maintain the medical equipment. Use the "Specific Training" section to identify how and when medical-equipment training will be provided to school staff.

Toileting and self-care are important aspects of the student's school day. Many students may be at risk for skin breakdown, constipation, or urinary tract infections if not properly managed during the school day. Discuss with the student's legal guardians the student's toileting needs. Note if the student needs assistance with toileting (i.e., catheterization) or if the student needs help with self-care (i.e., cleaning oneself, clothing management, and handwashing).

Indicate if the student needs physical assistance with feeding. The student may need a special feeding plan (i.e., g-tube feeds), which should be covered in the student's health plan. This section pertains to the level of assistance the student needs with feeding, such as assistance opening food containers, holding utensils, and so on.

Some students may have special diet restrictions. Consult with the student's legal guardians and medical providers to identify any eating or drinking precautions students may have. Items to consider include thickened liquids, special foods, significant food allergies, and so on. For example, some students with swallowing difficulties may have special drinking plans developed by their medical providers. Other students may only be allowed to drink water outside of mealtimes and only after brushing their teeth.

Assistance with mobility is another important section. Many students need assistance with shifting their weight and repositioning throughout the school day to prevent pressure injuries on the skin. Also, some students may use power wheelchairs, walkers, or special leg braces (i.e., ankle-foot orthosis) for mobility. Discuss with the student's legal guardians the type of mobility equipment the student may use during the school day and the type of support the student will need with mobility. Depending on the student's medical condition, the student may have restrictions on the amount of weight they are allowed to carry. Consult with the student's legal guardians and medical providers to assess if the student has weight restrictions. Some students may need assistance with carrying their textbooks, electronic devices, and other school materials.

Assistance with fine motor is another important area of consideration. Some students may need help with activities of daily living, and other students may need assistance with handwriting or typing. Indicate what type of support is needed for the student to complete fine-motor activities.

In the "Other" section, review any additional needs the student may have. For example, does the student need a special school evacuation plan in the event of a school emergency? It may be beneficial to complete the "School Day Needs Assessment" section to identify any additional support needs prior to completing this section (see table 5.1).

SPECIFIC TRAINING NEEDED

Table 5.1. School Day Needs Assessment

Activity	What student can do without assistance	What student cannot do and needs accommodations to complete	What student cannot do and needs assistance with	Areas to promote social acceptance and how peers will be used	Identify areas you will target for independence (should be identified in IEP)
Restroom/toileting	Able to use power wheelchair independently to transition to restroom at nurse's station.	Unable to transfer to toilet independently, needs mechanical lift for transfer.	Two adults needed to position student, assist with clothing, operate mechanical lift to toilet. Student able to sit independently on toilet once positioned.	Student needs extra time and privacy when using the restroom. The nurse's station restroom is appropriately equipped to accommodate student.	School-based OT and/or PT to provide training to staff on operating the mechanical lift, positioning the student on the toilet, and self-care needs. IEP goals will address the student's self-care needs.
Lunch	Able to use walker to ambulate to lunchroom with class.	Unable to verbalize food choices; needs picture menu with premade food choices; needs special fork, knife, spoon to eat lunch.	Adult needed to assist student with lunch tray while student uses walker in lunch line. Adult needed to open food containers and cut food for student.	Use peers to assist with lunch tray. Ensure that student is sitting with peers in the lunchroom.	School-based OT to identify fine-motor goals to assist student with opening food containers.

Detail the type of training needed and who will provide the training. For example, this section can be used to indicate the medical equipment that the student will need at school and the specific training necessary to monitor or adjust the student's medical equipment. Also, indicate training needed to safely position, transfer, or assist the student with mobility, toileting, and self-care. Identify the school personnel who will be trained. This section, as with all sections, should be modified if the student's medical or physical needs change.

NEXT STEPS REQUIRED

Is training required for staff, drivers, parents or guardians, and caregivers?

Yes

- Type of training needed:_____
- Participants: _____
- Date of training: _____

No

NEXT STEPS AND WHO IS RESPONSIBLE

Step to be Taken:	Responsible Party:

This section should be used to summarize action items that need to be completed and to identify individuals tasked with completing each action item. Do not assume that the student (and the staff) understands what is necessary for a safe environment for the student. Meet with the responsible staff to determine if any additional questions need to be addressed and whether the health care plan needs to be modified.

SCHOOL DAY NEEDS ASSESSMENT

Directions: Review the student's entire school day, and determine specifically what the student can or cannot do and the extent they need assistance.

Activity	What student can do without assistance	What student cannot do and needs accommodations to complete	What student cannot do and needs assistance with	Identify areas to promote social acceptance and how peers will be utilized	Identify areas you will target for independence (should be identified in IEP)

Detail the necessary steps, and put an approximate date for when the action item will be completed. For example, a student may need to use a mechanical lift to transfer in and out of their wheelchair for toileting and to perform self-care. An action item may be to identify school restrooms that would accommodate the student's personal care needs. Other students may need access to an elevator that requires a special pass or key to use. An action item may be to identify the staff member who would be responsible for issuing the elevator pass to the student.

List all aspects of the student's school day, starting from the moment the student enters the school building and ending when the student departs the building at the end of the school day. Consider such activities as passing periods, lunch, recess, restroom breaks, transitions within classrooms, seating needs, and so on. In some instances, it may be beneficial to observe the student over multiple days to document the student's school routine and identify activities the student completes daily.

Identify what the student can do without assistance from school staff. This section is very important because students should be as independent as possible in the school setting. For example, a student may need to use special equipment (i.e., a walker) with ambulation, but the walker allows the student to independently ambulate in the school building. Indicate any special equipment needed to allow for the student to be independent with the selected activity.

Identify what the student is unable to do and the special accommodations to complete the activity. Accommodations can be adaptations to the environment or special equipment for the student to complete the activity. For example, a student may need to use the elevator during passing periods, but the student is able to access the elevator independently. Other students may need special eating utensils during lunch or writing utensils for classwork, but they are able to eat and write independently with the special equipment. The goal for this section is to list the accommodations that the student needs so they can complete the activity as independently as possible.

Due to the student's medical condition, the student may not be able to complete the activity, and the student needs adult assistance to perform the activity safely. In this section, each activity should be reviewed for the appropriate level of adult assistance needed to perform the activity. For example, a student may be able to use special utensils independently during lunch, but the student is unable to open food containers or cut up food to bite-sized pieces. Use this section to break down the activity in steps needed to complete the activity, and assess the student's level of independence for each step or task. Indicate adult assistance only on the steps in which the student is unable to complete independently.

Peer socialization and peer groups are important aspects of school. It is very important that students with medical or health needs interact with their peers as much as possible. In some instances, it may be beneficial to incorporate a student's peers in the activity. For example, lunch and recess are two aspects of school in which peer socialization occurs naturally. A peer may be able to assist the student with their lunch tray in the cafeteria, or a peer may be able to carry the student's books in the hallways during passing periods. During the school-day assessment, look for opportunities to promote peer socialization and social acceptance of the student.

The final step in the school-day assessment is to identify areas that should be targeted for independence. This area should align with goals targeting independence in the student's IEP. School-based occupational therapists, physical therapists, and speech-language pathologists can play a vital role in identifying areas for student independence. For example, a school-based occupational therapist may target a student's fine-motor skills to enable a student to open food containers independently. A school-based physical therapist or occupational therapist can practice working on a student's transfer skills to allow for increased independence when using the restroom. School staff should invite the student's legal caregivers to share insights on the student's activities of daily living skills that may allow for increased independence in the school setting.

SUMMARY

This chapter provides a framework for the IEP team to consider the health and medical needs of an individual student. The assessment form is explained, with comments within each section. The nonannotated copy of the assessment is provided at the end of this chapter. As you consider health and medical needs as a related service, we hope the following questions are helpful for your thinking, procedures, and processes.

KEY TERMS

activities of daily living (ADLs): activities related to personal care, which can include bathing or showering, dressing, eating, walking, and toileting.
chronic health conditions: health conditions that last one year or more, require ongoing medical attention, or limit activities of daily living.
IEP team: the individualized education program (IEP) is developed by a team of people. IDEA requires certain team members, including a parent or

guardian, a general education teacher, a special education teacher, a school district representative, and an expert who can interpret the evaluation results. Others, such as related-service providers, should be invited based on the student's individualized needs.

least restrictive environment (LRE): a mandate in IDEA that students with disabilities should be educated to the maximum extent appropriate with their nondisabled peers.

QUESTIONS TO CONSIDER

1. What procedures are currently used by your district or division for developing health plans? How can you use the resources in this chapter in conjunction?
2. In your building, how are the school district or division emergency medical procedures and protocols shared with staff? For individual staff working with students who have health services, how are emergency procedures specific to that student shared?
3. How will information for a student's health services plan be shared with individuals working with the student? How will confidentiality be ensured?
4. What procedures exist for staff to ask questions and collaborate for students with health services?

MEDICAL AND HEALTH SUPPORTS

Date of meeting: _____

Name: _____

Age: _____

School: _____

Grade level: _____

Disability/disabilities: _____

Primary support: _____

Level of support: _____

Related services: _____

Date of last IEP revision: _____

School attendance:

- Regular school attendance
- Irregular school attendance (explain): _____
  _____
- Seasonal school attendance (explain): _____
  _____

Guardians' cell phone number(s): _____

Guardians' email address(es): _____

HEALTH SUPPORT

The student *needs* this type of aide, in accordance with a health services plan, to (check all that apply in the school setting):

- Monitor for seizure activity, vital signs, other medical symptoms, or drug side effects. Describe the nature of the activity or symptom for which monitoring is required and, if possible, the actual or expected frequency of such activity or symptoms: _____
  _____
- Medications administered at school: _____
- Implement emergency medical procedures pending arrival of nurse.
- Monitor or make routine adjustments to equipment. Describe the equipment in question: _____
- Assist with toileting or self-care.
- Assist with feeding.
- Nutrition/diet restrictions: _____
- Assist with mobility (wheelchair, walker, lift, positioning, etc.).
- Assist with fine motor (opening containers, writing, typing, etc.).
- Other (describe): _____

SPECIFIC TRAINING NEEDED

_____
_____
_____
_____
_____
_____
_____
_____

NEXT STEPS REQUIRED

Is training required for staff, drivers, parents or guardians, and caregivers?

Yes
- Type of training needed:_____
- Participants: _____
- Date of training: _____

No

NEXT STEPS AND WHO IS RESPONSIBLE

Step to be Taken:	Responsible Party:

SCHOOL DAY NEEDS ASSESSMENT

Directions: Review the student's entire school day, and determine specifically what the student can or cannot do and the extent they need assistance.

Activity	What student can do without assistance	What student cannot do and needs accommodations to complete	What student cannot do and needs assistance with	Identify areas to promote social acceptance and how peers will be utilized	Identify areas you will target for independence (should be identified in IEP)

Chapter Six

Roles of Related-Service Providers

Here it is: The chapter that sparked the idea for this entire book—what Lisa wished had existed when she was an SLP working in up to five buildings each school year and what she wished she had known as a special education case manager responsible for coordinating related services from providers she never saw in person. This conversation can feel very vulnerable to anyone and everyone who works in schools. Each of us brings skills and knowledge to the table, but none of us can possibly know everything the others have to offer. This is not a comparison game. Our hope here is to start conversations among the people who are all on the same team: those responsible for educating and supporting our students. The fact that some students need special education and related services is not a negative reflection on the classroom teacher or special education provider; it's a fact of the diversity of students we have the honor of teaching. The goal of special education and related-service provisions is to meet the needs of the students, through a collaborative effort by all the experts needed on the team: the classroom teacher, the special educator, and the related-service providers.

By now, you have a good sense of the important yet incredibly varied positive impact related-service providers can have on a student. You see there are myriad professionals trained to support students in accessing their education. You may be asking, "What else do they do?" and "How do I connect with them?" These are brilliant questions and, in this chapter, we offer some insight into how you can answer both. This is the heart of the matter, the value-add provided by related-service professionals to the IEP team, school staff, and larger educational community.

In addition to providing specific kinds of support for teachers and help for students, related-service personnel do the following (ASHA, 2015):

- provide prevention and intervention services in schools
- work to remove barriers to learning
- provide various instructional strategies
- work to improve classroom-management skills
- provide a continuum of support
- work with administrators
- consult with parents

In this chapter, we explore these topics within the context of five main related-service-provider roles: service provider, collaborator, professional expert, communicator, and IEP team member. We offer some examples throughout the chapter, again taken from our own experiences and communication with other teachers. You shouldn't be surprised that many examples involve an SLP because speech-language is the most common related service. This is Lisa's area of personal experience, and SLPs are among David's favorite providers to have testify in hearings because they tend to keep very good data. (Please note: In no way is this meant to discount the importance of other related-service personnel. Our examples are meant to support you in making connections to your own experiences through our experiences. We hope these connections then encourage you to spark a conversation with the related-service providers on your team.) We close out the chapter with some tips for effective communication and two "Day in the Life" snapshots from related-service providers currently working in schools: one in an elementary setting and one in a high school setting.

RELATED-SERVICE PROVIDERS AS, WELL, SERVICE PROVIDERS

Related-service providers are responsible for providing the services listed on the student's IEP. We discussed this in previous chapters and pointed out the type and amount of service is determined specifically for each eligible student. However, many educators don't know the various types of services that could be included. While not an exhaustive list (you knew we were going to say that, didn't you?), we discuss a few direct service options here.

Direct services means the related-service provider works directly with the student on the target skill or behavior. These services can occur individually with a student (often called one-to-one services), in small groups, or with the whole class. The location of these services can also vary, from a pull-out model in a special education setting to push-in model in a general education setting. With so much variability in what these services might look like, some examples might help. These are drawn from Lisa's experiences as a speech-language pathologist, but we didn't want to make this section about one person, so we use the *SLP* label here. Examples include the following:

- Individual, pull-out therapy to work on breath control for a voice disorder. This worked much better in a separate setting because some of the breath-control exercises were more effectively taught and practiced lying on the floor to isolate the push and pull of the diaphragm.
- Small-group, pull-out therapy to work on articulation skills. This allowed the SLP to work with several students at once, practicing sound production at various skill levels (isolation, initial word position, in phrases, etc.) while addressing listening practice, self-monitoring and correction skill work, and the bonus of some social skill work on taking turns, appropriate volume, and school-appropriate attention-gaining techniques. Many times, this therapy occurs within a "game" context, so the students see it as fun and stay motivated to engage. As is true with so much good teaching, small-group therapy can look like a simple game but includes intentional targeting of multiple skills. (Pro tip: If you see an educator or related-service professional playing a game with students, ask them about the skills they are addressing. They will likely enjoy sharing about their work, and you can pick up new ideas to incorporate into your teaching!)
- Small-group, push-in services in a classroom to support language skills required for mathematics. The SLP worked with students in a general education math classroom once a week. She supported the classroom teacher during whole-group instruction, then worked with a small group of students during independent work time, offering reteaching of concepts and additional practice with the language skills needed to solve multistep and word problems. This was a wonderful way to connect with multiple students and generalize therapy skills into the classroom setting. Even though they didn't have common planning time, the SLP and the classroom teacher met before school at least once a week to discuss lesson plans, instructional strategies, and data-collection methods.
- Coteaching to work on early literacy skills. The SLP was able to push into a kindergarten class twice a week and engage as one of the literacy centers. This required her to collaborate and plan with the teacher so they were working on the same skills, and it offered them the opportunity to embed effective therapy techniques into the general classroom, as the teacher would use some of the same strategies during instruction on days when the SLP was not in the room.

Before we move onto the next role, we hope you take a moment to review these examples, connect to your own experiences, and then consider these questions as starters:

- Have you worked with students who received direct services?
- Were there opportunities for you to discuss connections between these services and the work done in the classroom?
- Were the administrators in your building aware of the diverse services being offered to students?

We hope this information encourages you to ask your own questions and engage in new ways with the related-service providers on your team. When professionals continue to grow and work collaboratively, magic can happen for the students, professionals, and school community.

RELATED-SERVICE PROVIDERS AS COLLABORATORS

Collaboration is a commonly used word in education. Broadly defined, it usually means two or more people working together to achieve a goal or accomplish a task. Most teacher-preparation programs have at least one course on collaboration, but this typically focuses on collaboration within grade-level teams or the collaboration between the classroom teacher and the special educator. We encourage you to expand your definition of *collaboration* to include all the members of the team: classroom teachers, special educators, paraprofessionals, related-service providers, administrators, district support personnel . . . the list continues. As you expand your scope of collaborators, we also encourage you to consider different types of collaboration.

Related-service providers often are expected to engage in both formal and informal collaboration. Formal collaboration can be documented as consultation services on the IEP. As discussed in previous chapters, these services are designed to allow the related-service provider to offer training to the educators who work directly with the student. For example, when Lisa was the special education case manager for a student with vision impairment, that student's IEP included consultative services from the vision specialist, who taught Lisa how to use the magnification software and hardware the student used to access content. The vision specialist did not work directly with the student but was available to the educators in the building to offer training and technology support as needed.

Many educators interact with the related-service providers in informal ways, too. These are harder to capture for documentation purposes because they don't show up on the IEP, but they often are crucial to the success of implementing the student's IEP services. When teachers and related-service providers check in or touch base regularly, they have the opportunity to discuss effective ways to target IEP goals, develop data collection and progress-monitoring systems that can be applied across settings, and generally make the educational services more cohesive for the student. (Pro tip: When wanting to collaborate with related-service providers, ask what time or times work best for their busy schedules, which often include multiple buildings. Many providers are happy to have a phone conversation or meet virtually if face-to-face isn't an easy option.) When thinking about scheduling and collaborative work, it is great when teachers and related-service providers can document or schedule the time they spend communicating. Some teams mention this in the "Present Levels" section of the IEP, others are sure to address it with administration when building the school day schedule, and others may collaborate over a lunch period or planning time. While there is no formula for how to do this work, the informal consultation and collaborative communication among team members is a valuable part of the process.

As you reflect on this role of related-service providers as collaborators and consultants within your school, we encourage you to explore resources from the national organizations for the related-service professionals, such as the American Speech-Language Hearing Association (ASHA), the National Association of School Psychologists (NASP), and the American Occupational Therapy Association (AOTA), to name a few. You will find more about recommended resources in chapter 7. Often, these national organizations offer guidance on how to engage with school-based teams more effectively. For example, ASHA has information about interprofessional education (IPE) and interprofessional collaborative practice (IPCP) as consultative services. This fantastic resource provides education on creating an organized team and ways to include this intentional collaborative thinking into your daily work. As with any work we do in education, it's wonderful to recognize that different team members come from different perspectives and add value to the conversation.

RELATED-SERVICE PROVIDERS AS PROFESSIONAL EXPERTS

Just as classroom teachers are the experts in their content or grade-level curriculum, related-service providers are the experts in their fields. In earlier chapters, we shared examples of those providers and their professional training requirements. In the previous section, we highlight the role of the related-service provider as a trainer in relation to the goals and services written into the IEP. We encourage you to leverage the expertise of all members of your team beyond the IEP-specific consultation services. Related-service providers can be valuable resources to the entire school community, and the opportunities to connect with and educate other school staff are boundless. This might look like professional development with a school psychologist for a grade-level team to learn about implementing an instructional strategy with fidelity. Perhaps the orientation and mobility provider could offer a session to middle school administrators on basic safety factors to consider when determining the hallway traffic patterns during passing time. The school nurse could offer an informational session to the teachers and paraprofessionals who work with a student with seizures, so they are aware of proper safety protocols. The speech-language pathologist could train paraprofessionals on how to collect data for progress monitoring. Providing opportunities like these to share expertise elevates the role of the related-service provider from a student-specific role to one that is essential for creating a culture that benefits all students. (Pro tip: Ask your related-service providers if they have any feedback on trends or happenings they notice within the schools they service or across the district. From this conversation, could there be a staff professional-development opportunity from the related-service perspective?)

This collaboration should work both ways, too. We mentioned earlier how the classroom teacher is the content or curriculum expert. As the district adopts a new curriculum or grading scale, it would be wonderful for the classroom teachers to offer training sessions for the related-service providers so they are aware of these things, too. Remember: Everyone who works with the student is on the same team, and everyone has skills, talents, and knowledge to share. We hope these suggestions for using professional experts sparked additional ideas for you. Sharing expertise is a great way for teams to communicate more effectively, which can result in better educational opportunities for the students.

RELATED-SERVICE PROVIDERS AS COMMUNICATORS

By now, you should have a sense of how important effective communication is on a team. At the IEP-team level, it affects the quality and consistency of services provided to students. From the previous section, you can see that providing opportunities for related-service providers to communicate their expertise with all staff is beneficial to all students. Communication is crucial to the collaborative efforts of teams, from the IEP team to the building-level team to the greater school community. It is a powerful skill that should be practiced, respected, and reflected on continuously, both individually and as a team. Communication influences the opportunities team members have to learn with and from each other, as every team member brings something essential to the conversation. In this section, we want to specifically address ways the related-service providers can add value as communicators. Let's address this through a few different lenses:

Within the Team

Related-service providers can communicate with other team members about the specific related services the student should receive and their corresponding goals. You'll remember from an earlier chapter that all related services provided to a student with an IEP should be connected to a goal. The related-service professional is responsible for those goals, so that person is the point of contact for information about student progress toward the goals, how practice can be embedded into the classroom, and ideas for effective and efficient progress monitoring of goals. They are also very helpful in preparing the draft IEP and during the conversation at the IEP meeting (more on this later).

With Parents

The IEP team is responsible for providing IEP progress updates to parents on the same schedule as grade reporting. (Pro tip: Parent-teacher conferences can be a great time to connect outside the IEP meeting. Be sure to notify related-service providers of meeting dates and times in advance.) Because related-service providers are responsible for the goals connected to their services, they are great resources for how to share information with parents. They also are great at explaining some of the technical terms, or "alphabet soup," that are unique to their profession. We would want a vision expert to explain the results of a visual acuity test, and we would want an occupational therapist to answer questions about whether a habit is useful, dominating, or impoverished. We mentioned this earlier in the book, too, but in chapter 7, we offer some resources on the terminology, acronyms, and abbreviations of the various related services.

With External Service Providers

Just as you would want the related-service provider to explain domain-specific information to other team members and parents, they can be wonderful liaisons between the IEP team and external medical and therapeutic professionals. The IEP case manager and related-service provider can work together to glean information from outside evaluation reports and manage information requests from outside agencies.

With Administrators

Our approach here is a little different. While related-service providers can definitely be a value-add in conversations with administrators in many of the ways identified in the earlier "Within the Team" section, we really want to draw your attention to how administrators can support related-service providers. Often, related-service providers are assigned to buildings by district personnel, not chosen or hired directly by the building principal or building-level special education department chair. Additionally, the related-service provider could be assigned to multiple buildings or districts, allowing for minimal time in the building to develop community with the other team members. Beyond the obvious need to welcome the related-service provider to the team, include them in building-level communication, and develop a positive working relationship with them, here are some questions to consider:

- How are related-service personnel assigned to your school or district? If not by you, then how, when, and by whom will you be notified of a personnel change?
- What are your responsibilities for supervising the related-service providers? Who in the district is responsible for evaluating their performance? What are the evaluation metrics?
- What do the related-service providers need to know or consider as they navigate new teams and spaces? How can you support them as they join your building or district?

Having been a related-service provider assigned to different buildings each year, Lisa is very familiar with the "new guy" feeling that comes with not knowing the school building, culture, or community. It is difficult to do your best work in a building where, no matter how hard you try, you cannot seem to get people to collaborate with you on services for the students, where the only people who respond to your "hello" are the office secretary and the custodian, where you cannot find the teacher office supplies until February because no one thought to tell you about the special supply cabinet where they keep the only working stapler in the teacher work room. Empathy and awareness matter. Simple acts of kindness can make a lasting impression. One administrator offered a quick, 5-minute tour of the building, highlighting where the teacher bathrooms were, describing how to play nice with the copier so it wouldn't jam, and providing the master bell and specials schedule for the building. That simple gesture cost the principal literal minutes yet set a positive tone for the entire school year. It was a welcoming and inviting gesture that allowed Lisa to navigate the building more efficiently and map out her services schedule for that building much more effectively, saving hours of struggle. This was one building where she felt like part of the team. (Pro tip: Adding related-service providers to established social practices at your school promotes their inclusion into your community. This can look like making sure their email is on the all-staff list, adding birthdays to the social calendar, and having a name plate outside the space where they will primarily be working. These are simple but effective ways to affirm a related-service provider within the school culture.)

RELATED-SERVICE PROVIDERS AS IEP TEAM MEMBERS

In chapter 2, we addressed the required components of the IEP and the roles of the IEP team members. Here, we focus in on the value-add the related-service providers can offer within the IEP team. When the related-service providers have the opportunity to be active members of a school community and IEP team, they can support many aspects of the IEP process. Let's take a look at aspects related to the paperwork and the meeting.

IEP Paperwork

Anyone involved with special education knows IEP paperwork can feel daunting. There are many legally required components, and every team member has a role in completing the paperwork. Related-service providers have knowledge and expertise that should be used, especially when developing the present levels of academic and functional performance, goals, services, special considerations, accommodations, and modifications. If the student requires the related service of transportation (see chapter 4) or health care aides or supports (see chapter 5), then the related-service provider can offer insight into how those services should be structured, documented, and monitored for progress.

IEP Meeting

We've established the related-service providers as experts in their areas who are responsible for the goals and services connected to the documented related service. In an effective IEP team, the related-service provider can contribute before, during, and after the meeting. Prior to the meeting, the related-service provider can provide updates on progress toward current goals and recommendations for the next IEP meeting that can be included in the "Present Level" and "Goals" sections of the IEP document. At the meeting, the related-service provider can share information on student progress, answer questions specific to the related service provided from their professional expertise, offer clarification of terminology specific to that profession, and provide recommendations for goals and services to be included in the next IEP cycle. After the meeting, the related-service provider can communicate with the team about any updates or changes made to the services, goals, and strategies that can be incorporated into the student's educational plan. Communication is key here, as the IEP case manager will want to work with the related-service provider to ensure all involved staff are aware of the updates and changes and provided any additional needed information or training. The staff involved in implementing the IEP can include classroom teachers, special educators, and paraprofessionals, and it is important for the IEP team to have a process for collaborative communication so all are prepared to implement the IEP as written. (Pro tip: The related-service provider can provide context and support for *all* staff who will be working with a specific student. Anyone on the team can reach out. For example, the physical education teacher might want clarification from the physical therapist about how a student with an orthopedic impairment may engage in certain activities.)

TIPS FOR EFFECTIVE COMMUNICATION

We cover many aspects of effective communication throughout this book. Although, as noted, many different types of professionals work as related-service providers, and certain general principles apply to your interactions with them. Here are some general tips for working with related-service providers to consider (and potentially share with others on your team):

- Be welcoming. Many related-service providers travel from school to school. Do what you can to make them feel welcome at your school, and invite them to school activities. They are a part of the school. Make them feel that way.
- Collaborate. The related-service providers are working primarily with the student but will need to work with you to determine additional problems and successes. Talk with the related-service providers about your classroom schedule, the student's preferred activities, and aspects of the curriculum causing problems for the student. Share with them issues and concerns you may notice. Remember: You likely will be working with the student more hours per week than a related-service provider will. Talk with the provider about skills or strategies you should implement or any other follow-through activities you can provide for the student.

- Ask questions. Acknowledging their expertise is not a sign of your weakness—you're literally dealing with a different, individualized professional field, and that related-service provider can help you navigate the acronyms and technical terms. Asking questions not only promotes the student's learning but also can add skills to your toolbox. And these conversations can flow both ways, as the teacher can share content-specific information with the related-service provider.
- Treat them as professionals. Related-service providers have specific knowledge and skills in their area that can help the student make progress in the curriculum. They are a wonderful resource, and some of their suggestions for students with disabilities may actually help you with many other students in your classroom.
- Be specific. The classroom teacher often knows the student really well from the time they spend together. Being specific about what exactly a student is doing where, when, how often, and in what situations helps to better paint the picture for related-service providers about what is or isn't working.
- Suggest an observation. Invite the related-service providers to observe the student in the classroom and see how the student is functioning compared to peers.
- Be responsive. Respond promptly to related-service providers' questions and concerns and any requests for more information about how the student is doing.
- Schedule follow-up meetings. Whenever a related-service provider meets with the student, arrange a short meeting to make sure you are up to date about any issues or problems. Write down concerns to share at this meeting.
- Respect their time. Many related-service providers have heavy schedules and must work with multiple students within a short time frame. Respect this reality, and arrange meetings to talk with them about issues at times that are convenient for both of you.
- Share successes. Collaboration is joyful. Not only is sharing and celebrating a student's success bonding, but it also enhances the teamwork surrounding the student. It helps the student be fully seen by all members.

A DAY IN THE LIFE OF A RELATED-SERVICE PROVIDER

As we developed this chapter, we recognized the potential for overwhelm because there is so much to the various roles of a related-service provider. We wanted to share all this information in a way that was accessible and then have some sort of take-away or example to pull it all together. In conversations with classroom teachers about what could make this section better, we were given the idea to showcase a day in the life of a related-service provider (yet another example of how effective collaboration makes the end product better). We include a day in the life of Baleigh (table 6.1), an experienced SLP who currently works in an elementary school. We also have a day in the life of Mallory (table 6.2), a 1st-year SLP who works in a high school setting. As you read through these two examples, notice the similarities and differences in the types of services they provide across grade levels, the additional duties they engage in beyond service provision, and how they are connected to the school community.

A Day in the Life: Baleigh

First Name: Baleigh
Years of Experience: 5
Occupation: speech-language pathologist
Related Services Provided: speech therapy, language therapy
Settings Worked in and Currently Working in: elementary school with essential life skills program, skilled nursing facility (PRN)

The best part of my day is when: A student gets it for the first time. This could be the correct production of a targeted sound, following a two-step direction accurately, or answering a *wh-* question using their communication device for the first time. I love to celebrate successes with students and build them up to instill confidence and future success!

Table 6.1. A Day in the Life of Baleigh

Schedule	Summary of types of meetings, work, etc.
Start of the day	Meetings: SPED, CARE Team, Staff Meeting, Vision Team • Meetings in the mornings consist of a variety of functions, including behavior support, academic support, special education meetings, and staff meetings to address building needs. Hallway Duty/Breakfast Duty • Although this seems like another thing on my schedule, I love this part of the day. I get endless hugs from all students, some I see for services and some I don't. I get to tell them, "Good morning," and for some students, this is the first time they have heard it. It is a great way to start the day!
Morning	Articulation/Speech Therapy: Speedy Speech • My morning consists of seeing my "Speedy Speech" students. I implement five-minute speech sessions multiple days a week for most of my students with speech/articulation goals. We sit outside their regular education classroom and drill their targeted speech sounds. Using this approach, I am able to get lots of repetitions with students being out of their regular education classrooms for a short period of time. Students receive individual speech therapy services without having the lag period of travel down to my room.

Schedule	Summary of types of meetings, work, etc.
Morning (con't.)	Articulation/Speech Therapy: Speedy Speech • On Mondays, I check student speech folders, where they can earn prizes for completing and practicing their speech sounds at home. This is a great way to encourage carryover and also serves as communication between parents and me because they can write notes and let me know which words kids struggle with most. Their speech folders also include a "tips and tricks" section to help with sound elicitation.
Midday	Kindergarten Lunch Duty • Most of my lunch duty consists of opening milks and juice boxes, but it is such a great time to take a break from therapy sessions and enjoy conversations with kindergarteners. After lunch, I take them out to recess, where their classroom teachers pick them up. While they are going inside, I triage with several students about their behavior charts and goals for life. I ask them questions about their behavior and missing skills, and they respond. We talk about their behavior in lunch and at recess and what they did well or what they could have improved on for tomorrow. This time allows me to get to know students on a deeper level and develop relationships. Lunch • I grab my lunch from the lounge and head down to my room, where I enjoy some quiet time before my next group of students arrives. Language Groups • I see language groups for pull-out language therapy services after lunch. This group consists of students with various disabilities and diagnoses, including autism; specific learning disabilities; language impairments; other health impairments (ADHD, ADD, etc.); hearing impairments, and so on. This year my goal has been to incorporate language goals into various literacy units. I incorporate a book related to topics students are learning about in their general education classrooms or seasonal books into every session. One day a week, this session consists of a pragmatics/social skills lesson, where we discuss social stories and various situational questions. Triage • Students come down to my room at this time to triage. Triage can include asking them questions regarding their missing skills related to behaviors, drilling letter names/sounds, and so on. I collect data every week with these students and report back to the CARE team (academic intervention team) to determine where students need extra support and discuss progress. Plan Time • This time consists of making quick parent phone calls, answering emails, or planning for future therapy sessions.

(continued)

Table 6.1. *(continued)*

Schedule	Summary of types of meetings, work, etc.
Afternoon	Push-In Rotations/Whole-Group Language and Speech Therapy in Essential Life Skills Special Education Rooms (3rd- through 5th-Grade Rooms) <ul><li>I service students in our Essential Life Skills Program at this time. These students have an array of diagnoses and disability areas, including autism, intellectual disabilities, down syndrome, orthopedic impairments, cerebral palsy, and more. Some students use verbalizations to communicate; others use assistive technology devices (iPads with communication apps, switches, static voice-output devices) and picture exchange. For these sessions, I have to be sure every student has a way to respond to my various questions and activities. I typically add and program vocabulary into their devices for the week if I need to incorporate specific fringe vocabulary related to topics.</li><li>Monday through Thursdays consist of what we call "rotations." Four adults each have a station: special education teacher, me (SLP), occupational therapist, and paraprofessional. I have a PowerPoint displayed on the board with a visual schedule of who each student is with for every rotation. Stations last for 10 minutes each, then students rotate around the room. Students travel with a star chart to each station. Adults give the students a star if they worked hard and tried their best throughout the rotation. After rotations, we gather as a group on the carpet to see how everyone did. We celebrate successes in our rotations.</li><li>On Fridays, I do a whole-group language therapy session. I start these sessions with going over a visual schedule of our agenda. We begin with a greetings song, where students are able to echo the song and sing along. Then, we move onto discussing feelings, read a book, then complete the activity I have planned. These consist of hands-on activities.</li></ul> Push-In Rotations/Whole-Group Language and Speech Therapy in Essential Life Skills Special Education Rooms (Kindergarten through 2nd-Grade Rooms) <ul><li>This time has the same set-up as the older essential life skills class. I do rotations Monday through Thursday and a whole-group language therapy session on Fridays.</li></ul>
End of the day	Language Therapy Groups <ul><li>I end the day with a small-group language therapy session. These students are older, so their goals and our focus are typically on more higher-level language skills, including figurative language and more advanced vocabulary and semantics concepts.</li></ul> Car Rider Duty <ul><li>I assist kindergarten students in getting down to the gym for car riders. This is another opportunity where I get to make connections and form relationships with all students at the school and their families.</li></ul> Tutoring <ul><li>After school, I pull two students from our after-school program to do tutoring in reading. We focus on phonics, phonemic awareness, and overall reading skills in order to reinforce concepts learned in the general education classroom.</li></ul>

One thing I'd like others to know about my job: I want others to know that speech and language skills are underlying deficits for so many students who struggle with academics, especially in reading and writing. Articulation deficits affect a child's ability to accurately produce sounds and therefore affect the ability to identify and use letter sounds and names, segment and decode words, and have overall phonemic awareness skills. Spoken language also is the foundation for reading and writing. Students with weaker oral language skills and overall comprehension are more likely to show difficulties with literacy and reading comprehension. Working as an IEP team (including the SLP) will benefit the child in all areas of academics.

A Day in the Life: Mallory

First Name: Mallory
Years of Experience: 0; 1st-year speech-language pathologist
Occupation: speech-language pathologist, freshman girls' basketball coach
Related Services Provided: speech therapy, language therapy
Settings Worked in and Currently Working in: high school special education
   department (essential life skills program, cotaught classrooms, resource
   classrooms, and applied classrooms)

The best part of my day is when: A student is excited to be able to spend time working on their goals in speech or language therapy. Even when a student walks into the room not motivated or in a bad mood, if I am able to motivate them or at least make them smile, this is the best part of my days.

Table 6.2. A Day in the Life of Mallory

Schedule	Summary of types of meetings, work, etc.
Start of the day	Hallway Duty • Supervision of hallway and students, stand in the hallways between bathrooms and stairs to ensure students are walking to class
Morning	Essential Life Skills Group (Push into Classroom for Language Therapy on Mondays and Wednesdays and Pull Out for Language Therapy on Tuesdays and Fridays) • I have two students in this classroom at one time. I sit between both students. One student uses Proloquo2go on their iPad, while the other uses a two-switch talker with "Yes" on the left button and "No" on the right button. • Assist students in class while using their assistive technology devices. Ensure they are able to find key concepts and definitions on their devices, and allow them to participate in class. • Use "My turn," "Yes/no," and vocabulary words.

(continued)

Table 6.2. *(continued)*

Schedule	Summary of types of meetings, work, etc.
Morning (con't.)	Language Therapy • Two groups in the morning consist of students with varying disabilities, including autism; language impairment; other health impaired (ADHD, ADD, etc.). • Both groups have semantics and syntax goals. Therapy will include homework from their English class (English I, II, or Senior Literature and Composition) • Therapy consists of breaking down readings and determining the main ideas of paragraphs to better understand the meaning of the entire reading or book. As a group, we underline unknown words and use context clues to understand the meaning. • Syntax consists of any type of writing they are working on in class. If they are not writing that day, then I have activities, as well. This may include having a short writing prompt and the students using a graphic organizer to tell the beginning, middle, and end of a story.
Midday	Response to Intervention (RTI) • As of right now, I see two students for language RTI. I pull these two students out of their skills support class (study hall for students in special education) so they will not miss anything in their core classes. This group will work on skills that teachers or parents have concerns about or have seen them struggle with in class. I see students for RTI when they are under an evaluation. Once I give my data to the team for the results meeting, they can decide if we want to continue with RTI services or provide language services through an IEP. Lunch • I grab my lunch from the refrigerator and head back to my room. Teachers who have the same lunch period as I do will come into my room, as well. Plan Time • This time consists of making quick parent phone calls, answering emails, planning for future therapy sessions, or completing IEPs.
Afternoon	Speedy Speech/Speech Therapy • In the afternoon, I see three students for "Speedy Speech." Because I work at a high school, there are not many students I see for speech therapy. Most have been released from speech therapy before they go to high school. I pull these three students from a class and into the hallway. I have an iPad that has their targeted sounds. The app on the iPad can categorize the words into initial, medial, and final position, as well as words, phrases, and sentences. This way they are able to get through more words with the swipe of a finger across the screen.

Schedule	Summary of types of meetings, work, etc.
Afternoon (con't.)	Consult Minutes • Some of my students are on "consult" minutes. This means I only see a student for 5 to 10 minutes a week. Most of my students who are on consult will need check-ins or reminders for social situations or how to respond to situations that have happened throughout the school day. The other three students who are on consult use AT devices. During this time, I check in with teachers about new vocabulary words that I need to add or address concerns with teachers about the student or their device.
End of the day	Language Therapy Groups • I end the day with two small-group language therapy sessions. These students are older, so their goals and our focus are typically on higher-language skills, including figurative language and more advanced vocabulary and semantics concepts. This time is used to catch up on ELA homework or ask questions about classwork that they do not understand. Practice/Game Day • Every day after school, I coach the freshman girls' basketball team. We practice from an hour and a half to two hours. If it is a game day, the athletes go to the gym, and we go over plays and drills to prepare for the game. We then get on the bus to head to the game.

One thing I'd like others to know about my job: **Speech-language pathologists do so much more than just telling a student to say this sound correctly. We help students learn social skills and how to relay their emotions, understand grade-level text, and most importantly be able to communicate in the best way they can. Most of the time, we are more than SLPs. We are counselors, teachers, confidants, and nurses. We have to make decisions fast and do what is best for our students.**

SUMMARY

Related-service providers serve many roles in the IEP and school teams. Their professional skills, coupled with the professional skills of the classroom teachers and other educators in the building, can result in more effective instruction for students. When all members of the team are encouraged to communicate and be collaborative, all service providers are better informed, instructional practices and learning environments improve, and there are better conversations among team members. These better practices result in more advocacy for and ability to meet the needs of the students we serve.

KEY TERMS

collaboration: two or more people working together to achieve a goal or accomplish a task.
consultation: related-service providers provide training to educators who work directly with a student.
coteaching: a collaborative approach to instruction in which two professionals work together to plan and implement instruction, usually for a class that includes students with special education services.
individualized education program (IEP): a legal document between the school district and the parents or guardians that defines special education services for an individual child eligible to receive special education; also individualized education *plan*.
related services: transportation and such developmental, corrective, and other supportive services required to help a child with a disability benefit from special education.
value-add: something or someone who adds value and benefits the team, project, or purpose.

QUESTIONS TO CONSIDER

1. What do services look like for related-service providers within your building? In what settings do they occur? What does this tell you about least restrictive environment (LRE) in your school, district, or division?
2. At the IEP team level, what are you doing well in terms of both the paperwork process and team membership? Upon reflection, what are areas of growth?
3. What interdisciplinary conversations are happening at both the student and school levels?
4. What action steps will be taken (individually, as a team, as a school) to better recognize and use related-service providers within the school community?
5. What procedures and resources are in place when you or other team members have a question about a related service provided to your student(s)?
6. What opportunities do you currently offer related-service providers to connect with school staff, both personally and professionally?
7. How do you plan to include the related-service providers in your work with students, both daily and generally? How can you specifically support each other's efforts?
8. Which effective communication tips resonated with you as strengths, both personally and within your school team? Which tips resonated with you as areas to develop?

Chapter Seven

Recommended Resources

By this point in the book, we are confident you understand that related services are important components of the IEP for some students to support their ability to access and benefit from special education and to receive a free appropriate public education. We also are sure you see the value-add of the related-service providers to the IEP team and school community. And as is the case with any learning we do with students and within education, we are equally confident you have additional questions and need additional resources as you continue your collaborative learning and work with related-service providers. Please use the resources in this chapter to help you continue that important work!

We organize the resources by type and task. The first section is a list of books you may want to explore, either individually or as part of your team, as you deepen your knowledge about how to support students who receive special education. The next section is an easy reference list of many of the national organizations for the professionals involved in providing related services. Their websites offer great information that can be helpful to you and your IEP team. Third, we provide some online resources for you to continue your own learning and find resources to share with others on your team. These resources work well for professional development and for sharing with families, educators, administrators, and even school board members. The fourth section is something you may not have seen before: the complete wording of the section of the regulations for related services. Finally, we have some words of advice regarding related services.

BOOKS

There are numerous books and journal articles about special education written in the last half-century. As you continue your learning in this area, please note that some of these texts are written for different audiences and from different perspectives. In our work with teachers and preservice teachers, we have found a good place to start is with books or articles written for teachers. In the literature, these are often referred to as "practitioner" texts. In fact, David has been involved in writing several practitioner texts to meet the needs of educators, special educators, and administrators. (Full disclosure: You'll notice his name on some books mentioned in this chapter.) Here are some of the practitioner texts we use regularly for both preservice teacher preparation and in-service professional development:

A Teacher's Guide to Special Education, by David F. Bateman and Jenifer L. Cline, is a guide for classroom teachers on their roles and responsibilities in the education of students with disabilities. It offers instructional best practices for the classroom.

Special Education Law Case Studies: A Review from Practitioners, by David F. Bateman, Jenifer L. Cline, and Jonathan D. Steele, is collection of case studies to support new and experienced special educators and leaders as they work to provide appropriate services to students with disabilities. Each case includes multiple perspectives to support the reader in understanding complex situations more fully.

The Essentials of Special Education Law, by Andrew M. Markelz and David F. Bateman, was written for educators, administrators, and families to be a concise yet comprehensive resource for understanding special education law.

What Really Works with Exceptional Learners, edited by Wendy Murawski and Kathy Lynn Scott, is a reader-friendly resource on evidence-based practices and is designed to empower the reader in supporting students with special education services.

Developing Educationally Meaningful and Legally Sound IEPs, by Mitchell L. Yell, David F. Bateman, and James G. Shriner, was written for IEP teams to support their use of better practices to develop IEPs that are both educationally meaningful for the student and legally sound. It includes multiple forms and graphics to support the IEP team in developing and documenting the student's special education program.

Of course, there are other wonderful books out there and we encourage you to explore titles that will support your ongoing learning as you work to support students with special education needs. As you find new resources, be sure to apply the better-practice standards and use resources firmly grounded in effective practices, solid research, and a clear understanding of the law.

NATIONAL ORGANIZATIONS AND RESOURCES FOR RELATED-SERVICE PROVIDERS

In this section, we provide information about some national organizations for the professionals responsible for related services. These organizations offer guidance for best practices for the professionals and often have resources directly addressing the provision of services in school settings. We use the same grouping structure here that is found in chapter 3: "Communication Services"; "Physical Services"; "Social, Emotional, and Psychological Services"; and "Medical and Health Services."

Communication Services

- The American Speech-Language-Hearing Association (ASHA, www.asha.org) provides guidance and national certification for both audiologists and speech-language pathologists.
- The National Council on Interpreting in Health Care (NCIHC, www.ncihc.org) provides a resource to connect with interpreter associations across the United States.

Physical Services

- American Occupational Therapy Association (AOTA, www.aota.org)
- American Physical Therapy Association (APTA, www.apta.org)
- National Council for Therapeutic Recreation Certification (NCTRC, www.nctrc.org)
- The National Federation for the Blind (NFB, www.nfb.org) provides resources related to orientation and mobility services.

Social, Emotional, and Psychological Services

- American School Counselor Association (ASCA, www.schoolcounselor.org)
- National Association of School Psychologists (NASP, www.nasponline.org)
- School Social Work Association of America (SSWAA, www.sswaa.org)

Medical and Health Services

- American Academy of Pediatrics (AAP, www.aap.org)
- National Association of School Nurses (NASN, www.nasn.org)

ONLINE RESOURCES

A quick internet search reveals numerous sites devoted to special education. Here are some evidence-based sites and quality resources we share often with educators and preservice teachers:

- The sheer number of acronyms and abbreviations related to special education and disabilities can be daunting. While there are several lists available, we often share this list provided by the Center for Parent Information and Resources (https://www.parentcenterhub.org/acronyms/).
- IRIS's module *IEPs: Developing High-Quality Individualized Education Programs* details the process of developing high-quality individualized education programs (IEPs) for students with disabilities. The module discusses the requirements for IEPs as outlined in the Individuals with Disabilities Education Act (IDEA), with implications of the Supreme Court's ruling in *Endrew F. v. Douglas County School District* (estimated module completion time: 3 hours; https://iris.peabody.vanderbilt.edu/module/iep01/).
- IRIS's module *IEPs: How Administrators Can Support the Development and Implementation of High-Quality IEPs* is specifically designed with school administrators in mind. This module offers guidance on how to support and facilitate the development and implementation of high-quality IEPs, including the monitoring of student progress (estimated module completion time: 2 hours; https://iris.peabody.vanderbilt.edu/module/iep02/).
- Misunderstood Minds is a collection of resources provided by the Public Broadcasting Service (PBS) as a companion site to their documentary on learning differences and disabilities. This website includes information on the documentary, as well as simulations for people to explore and experience the impact different academic and attentional difficulties may have on learning (https://www.pbs.org/wgbh/misunderstoodminds/).
- Understood.org is dedicated to helping those who learn and think differently discover their potentials, take control, find community, and stay on positive paths along each stage of life's journey. These resources are accessible to a variety of audiences and serve as great materials to share with parents, teachers, paraprofessionals, and community members interested in supporting students with disabilities (https://www.understood.org/).

THE REGULATIONS FOR RELATED SERVICES

In this book, we mention more than once the federal regulations that outline the requirements for provision of related services. We realize many educa-

tors may not have seen the actual language in the regulations, so we include it here for your reference. The complete law and regulations can be found at www.sites.ed.gov.
Sec. 300.34 Related services
Statute/Regs Main » Regulations » Part B » Subpart A » Section 300.34
Sec. 300.34 Related services

a. General. Related services means transportation and such developmental, corrective, and other supportive services as are required to assist a child with a disability to benefit from special education, and includes speech-language pathology and audiology services, interpreting services, psychological services, physical and occupational therapy, recreation, including therapeutic recreation, early identification and assessment of disabilities in children, counseling services, including rehabilitation counseling, orientation and mobility services, and medical services for diagnostic or evaluation purposes. Related services also include school health services and school nurse services, social work services in schools, and parent counseling and training.
b. Exception; services that apply to children with surgically implanted devices, including cochlear implants.
   1. Related services do not include a medical device that is surgically implanted, the optimization of that device's functioning (e.g., mapping), maintenance of that device, or the replacement of that device.
   2. Nothing in paragraph (b)(1) of this section—
      i. Limits the right of a child with a surgically implanted device (e.g., cochlear implant) to receive related services (as listed in paragraph (a) of this section) that are determined by the IEP Team to be necessary for the child to receive FAPE.
      ii. Limits the responsibility of a public agency to appropriately monitor and maintain medical devices that are needed to maintain the health and safety of the child, including breathing, nutrition, or operation of other bodily functions, while the child is transported to and from school or is at school; or
      iii. Prevents the routine checking of an external component of a surgically implanted device to make sure it is functioning properly, as required in §300.113(b).
c. Individual related services terms defined. The terms used in this definition are defined as follows:
   1. Audiology includes—
      i. Identification of children with hearing loss;

ii. Determination of the range, nature, and degree of hearing loss, including referral for medical or other professional attention for the habilitation of hearing;
iii. Provision of habilitative activities, such as language habilitation, auditory training, speech reading (lip-reading), hearing evaluation, and speech conservation;
iv. Creation and administration of programs for prevention of hearing loss;
v. Counseling and guidance of children, parents, and teachers regarding hearing loss; and
vi. Determination of children's needs for group and individual amplification, selecting and fitting an appropriate aid, and evaluating the effectiveness of amplification.
2. Counseling services means services provided by qualified social workers, psychologists, guidance counselors, or other qualified personnel.
3. Early identification and assessment of disabilities in children means the implementation of a formal plan for identifying a disability as early as possible in a child's life.
4. Interpreting services includes—
i. The following, when used with respect to children who are deaf or hard of hearing: Oral transliteration services, cued language transliteration services, sign language transliteration and interpreting services, and transcription services, such as communication access real-time translation (CART), C-Print, and TypeWell; and
ii. Special interpreting services for children who are deaf-blind.
5. Medical services means services provided by a licensed physician to determine a child's medically related disability that results in the child's need for special education and related services.
6. Occupational therapy—
i. Means services provided by a qualified occupational therapist; and
ii. Includes—
A. Improving, developing, or restoring functions impaired or lost through illness, injury, or deprivation;
B. Improving ability to perform tasks for independent functioning if functions are impaired or lost; and
C. Preventing, through early intervention, initial or further impairment or loss of function.
7. Orientation and mobility services—
i. Means services provided to blind or visually impaired children by qualified personnel to enable those students to attain systematic

orientation to and safe movement within their environments in school, home, and community; and
ii. Includes teaching children the following, as appropriate:
   A. Spatial and environmental concepts and use of information received by the senses (such as sound, temperature and vibrations) to establish, maintain, or regain orientation and line of travel (e.g., using sound at a traffic light to cross the street);
   B. To use the long cane or a service animal to supplement visual travel skills or as a tool for safely negotiating the environment for children with no available travel vision;
   C. To understand and use remaining vision and distance low vision aids; and
   D. Other concepts, techniques, and tools.
8.
   i. Parent counseling and training means assisting parents in understanding the special needs of their child;
   ii. Providing parents with information about child development; and
   iii. Helping parents to acquire the necessary skills that will allow them to support the implementation of their child's IEP or IFSP.
9. Physical therapy means services provided by a qualified physical therapist.
10. Psychological services includes—
    i. Administering psychological and educational tests, and other assessment procedures;
    ii. Interpreting assessment results;
    iii. Obtaining, integrating, and interpreting information about child behavior and conditions relating to learning;
    iv. Consulting with other staff members in planning school programs to meet the special educational needs of children as indicated by psychological tests, interviews, direct observation, and behavioral evaluations;
    v. Planning and managing a program of psychological services, including psychological counseling for children and parents; and
    vi. Assisting in developing positive behavioral intervention strategies.
11. Recreation includes—
    i. Assessment of leisure function;
    ii. Therapeutic recreation services;
    iii. Recreation programs in schools and community agencies; and
    iv. Leisure education.
12. Rehabilitation counseling services means services provided by qualified personnel in individual or group sessions that focus specifically

on career development, employment preparation, achieving independence, and integration in the workplace and community of a student with a disability. The term also includes vocational rehabilitation services provided to a student with a disability by vocational rehabilitation programs funded under the Rehabilitation Act of 1973, as amended, 29 U.S.C. 701 et seq.
13. School health services and school nurse services means health services that are designed to enable a child with a disability to receive FAPE as described in the child's IEP. School nurse services are services provided by a qualified school nurse. School health services are services that may be provided by either a qualified school nurse or other qualified person.
14. Social work services in schools includes—
    i. Preparing a social or developmental history on a child with a disability;
    ii. Group and individual counseling with the child and family;
    iii. Working in partnership with parents and others on those problems in a child's living situation (home, school, and community) that affect the child's adjustment in school;
    iv. Mobilizing school and community resources to enable the child to learn as effectively as possible in his or her educational program; and
    v. Assisting in developing positive behavioral intervention strategies.
15. Speech-language pathology services includes—
    i. Identification of children with speech or language impairments;
    ii. Diagnosis and appraisal of specific speech or language impairments;
    iii. Referral for medical or other professional attention necessary for the habilitation of speech or language impairments;
    iv. Provision of speech and language services for the habilitation or prevention of communicative impairments; and
    v. Counseling and guidance of parents, children, and teachers regarding speech and language impairments.
16. Transportation includes—
    i. Travel to and from school and between schools;
    ii. Travel in and around school buildings; and
    iii. Specialized equipment (such as special or adapted buses, lifts, and ramps), if required to provide special transportation for a child with a disability

WORDS OF ADVICE

Often, textbooks or education-related websites have a section of frequently asked questions (FAQ). Because this book is a conversation with you, the reader, we offer instead some words of advice—a final set of tips, ideas, or suggestions, if you will. We provide these words of advice as numbered items with topic headings to support organization and an easy review when you come back to this chapter again.

Related-Service Words of Advice

1. General Educators and Related Services

Because most students with disabilities spend most of their time in the general educational classroom, it is imperative to have the general education teacher in the meeting when discussing the needs of the students and whether related services are necessary. Make sure they attend and are able to participate.

2. General Education and Related Services

To receive related services, a student must be eligible for special education. It is required that a general education teacher participate in the selection of evaluation components for an initial or a triennial reevaluation.

3. General Education and Related Services

General education teachers should have training so they know the purpose of the testing—to identify any disabilities, to determine current educational needs and current academic achievement, and to determine any need for special education and related services. The general education teacher's input is particularly important when the team is determining the ability of the student to participate in the general education curriculum. Without this background information that can be provided through a review of the regulations or other training, the general education teacher will have a hard time understanding their role in the special education process. If the general education teacher does not have this training as a part of their preservice instruction, then it should be provided as a part of a district onboarding process.

4. Principals and Related Services

An administrator, often a principal, is responsible for compliance in the building with students receiving the special education and related services that are delineated in their respective IEPs. If the administrator has not had adequate training on special education as part of their administrator-certification program, then they should seek it out as part of their continued professional development.

5. Principals and Related Services

Typically, principals must ensure that adequate and trained special education teachers, related-service providers, and other staff are provided to the building to meet special education timelines and requirements.

6. Principals and Related Services

If there is ever a complaint, a due-process hearing, or a request for mediation where noncompliance is a potential issue, the principal should be knowledgeable about the procedures used in their building and be able to explain how the related services were provided, along with the specifics for the students.

7. Related-Services Eligibility

All students are determined eligible for special education *and* related services through a team decision. It is not one person who makes the determination or overrules the team.

8. Related-Services Eligibility

The need for related services under IDEA is determined by the IEP team. A school team should not use the eligibility process to determine if the student qualifies for a related service. The determination of related-services needs comes *after* eligibility for special education. It is the IEP team who discusses and decides the need for a particular related service.

9. Related-Services Eligibility

The list of related services under the regulations and those covered in this book are not exhaustive. It depends on the needs of the student. Other services may qualify as related services even though not listed in the definition. The IEP team makes the determination of what related services are needed.

10. Related-Services Eligibility

Related services are provided under IDEA when the student is identified with a disability and receives special education services, and the related service is required to be added to the IEP for the student to benefit. The IEP team must find the particular related service is necessary for FAPE and in support of the special education services required by the student.

11. Related Services and Medical Issues

Services provided by a doctor are medical services and not required as a related service (see the discussion of the *Garret F.* Supreme Court case in Appendix B).

12. Related Services and Medical Issues

Services provided by a nurse, if required for the student with disabilities to attend school, may qualify as a related service.

13. Related Services and Cost

Cost is not part of the definition of a related service. As a result, costly nursing services required for the student to attend school may be a related service and are not excluded as a medical service.

14. Related Services and Benefit

The focus of all discussions on the need for related services should always start with whether it is necessary for the student to receive FAPE. Do not focus the IEP discussion of the need for a related service solely on the benefit that the student will receive from the provision of the related service. Most related services would be beneficial for any student, but the test for their provision is not whether they are beneficial but whether they are needed for FAPE.

15. Related Services and Doctors Notes

The determination about the need for a related service is an IEP team decision. It is not the determination of anyone from outside the school setting. Therefore, related services are not provided solely on the basis that a doctor or treating psychiatrist or psychologist has prescribed the service for the child with a disability. The information provided by the professional *must* be considered, but the recommendation is not determinative of the need for the related service from an educational perspective.

16. Related Services and Scheduling

Document the provision of the related service in the amount specified in the IEP. The frequency and scheduling of the services should be noted, as well as the knowledge or skills addressed during sessions and progress monitoring of student performance. This information will provide proof of IEP implementation in the event of a challenge. The related-service provider must also document the implementation of related-service goals and objectives and the collection of data or information so that progress reports can be provided to parents or guardians.

17. Related Services and Scheduling

The amount of time a student receives a related service should be based on the need of the student, not on what is available in the district. Additionally, the schedule of the day *does not* dictate the amount of services, nor does the volume of the related-service provider's caseload.

18. Related Service and IEP meetings

The related-service provider is not a required participant in the IEP meeting. The related-service provider should be invited to the IEP meeting in many cases so the IEP team has the information it needs about the amount of related services to provide and needed goals. If the related-service provider is not present at the IEP meeting, then the IEP team *must* be prepared to discuss related services by being knowledgeable about the student's continued need for and current performance in the related service.

19. Related-Services Changes

Parental or guardian consent is required to conduct an evaluation and to make changes to the IEP, including a change to the related services.

20. Related-Services Percentages

Explain placement terms to parents or guardians, such as *pull-out, resource room,* or *percentages*. The more a parent or guardian understands about what is provided, the better they can be a part of the team considering programming and placement for the child.

KEY TERMS

free appropriate public education (FAPE): the education to which every student is entitled under IDEA. Every student is entitled to an education that is appropriate for their unique needs and that is provided at no cost to the parents or guardians.

IEP team: the team of people who develop the individualized education program (IEP). IDEA requires certain team members, including a parent or guardian, a general education teacher, a special education teacher, a school district representative, and an expert who can interpret the evaluation results. Others, such as related-service providers, should be invited based on the student's individualized needs.

Individuals with Disabilities Education Act (IDEA): a law that guarantees educational rights to all students with disabilities and makes it illegal for school districts to refuse to educate a student based on their disability.

least restrictive environment (LRE): a mandate in IDEA that students with disabilities should be educated to the maximum extent appropriate with their nondisabled peers.

medical services: services that can only be provided by a licensed physician; exempt from the definition of related services, unless needed for diagnostic or evaluative purposes.

regulations: instructions written by the executive branch that provide direction on how to implement and enforce laws passed by Congress. Special educators must be aware of federal and state regulations pertaining to special education law.

related services: transportation and such developmental, corrective, and other supportive services required to help a child with a disability benefit from special education.

special education: education specially designed to meet the unique needs of a child with a disability.

value-add: something or someone who adds value and benefits the team, project, or purpose.

QUESTIONS TO CONSIDER

1. Are there some books on the list in this chapter you have read before? If so, what new information can you gain from them as you consider your new learning about related services?
2. Is there a book in the list that stood out as a "next read" for you, either as an individual or as a team?

3. What professional-development opportunities would you like to have in conjunction with the book(s)?
4. Within the list of national organizations, which one(s) stood out to you as a resource you would like to explore first?
5. Is there a particular student who comes to mind when thinking about related services and the professional guidance you've received from their provider(s) on working with students in schools?
6. Review the case studies of Max, Saraiah, and Angelus. What questions do you have? Which national organizations would you want to explore for more information about the related services needed for each student?
7. Which online resources are familiar to you? How might you view them differently from the perspective of related services?
8. Which type of online information or learning is most appealing to you (e.g., modules, simulations, parent-friendly language)? What specific knowledge or skills would help you as you think about supports for your students with disabilities?
9. Now empowered with the knowledge of what the regulations say about what related-service providers do, how has your perspective on related services changed?
10. What questions do you still have about the regulations? What resources (people, books, websites) can you access to answer those questions?
11. Which words of advice stood out to you? Were you able to connect each one back to a section of the book?
12. How has the knowledge about the importance of related services affected your understanding of special education, LRE, and FAPE?

Appendix A

Case Studies

CASE STUDY 1: MAX

Max is a 6-year-old 1st-grade student attending his local elementary school. During the kindergarten screening in the April prior to his attending school, the evaluator noticed Max had difficulty saying multiple letter sounds, including /l/, /k/, and /g/. Max's parents also noted he was unable to say the name of the family dog, Laika, instead calling the dog "Yaida." As a result of the screening, Max was referred for a speech and language evaluation. The evaluation was completed in August of his kindergarten year, with Max meeting eligibility for special education for speech impairment. The evaluation showed no concerns in vision or hearing, as Max passed screening for both and had no history of ear infections and had appropriate receptive language skills and appropriate preacademic skills. The IEP team, including the speech-language pathologist (SLP), the parents, the principal, and the classroom teacher, met to develop the program, writing an IEP that included speech therapy services from an SLP twice weekly, each time for 20 minutes. One weekly session was an individual session, the other was a small-group session.

As Max started 1st grade, the IEP team met again for the annual IEP review. The SLP shared Max's progress toward his speech goal, noting he is now able to produce the /k/ and /g/ sounds correctly in isolation and initial word position during sessions, but this skill has not yet generalized to other settings. The teacher noted concerns with how Max's speech is affecting his ability to decode words in reading and to spell phonetically in writing. Max can read his own writing with matching detailed illustrations but often needs extended time to explain and talk through the writing so the teacher can fully comprehend his meaning. At this time, despite the noted errors, Max is not demonstrating frustration or avoidance when asked to read, write, or spell. The teacher often asks Max to repeat what he says for clarity, in both academic and social situations. In fact, she has taught the class routines for requesting or providing clarity, which help many students who need additional time or practice in clearly expressing their thoughts verbally.

The IEP team discussed the need for continued services in speech, both for articulation and impact on literacy, as well as other possible supports for Max. The SLP and teacher recommended continuing the pull-out speech therapy twice weekly and adding push-in services during reading and writing time. The following are some recommendations the team identified as ways everyone on the team can support Max:

- Model correct pronunciation without overtly correcting his articulation errors.
- Give extra time to share ideas and communicate.
- Be patient when he speaks or reads aloud, avoiding the temptation to finish sentences for him.

Questions to Consider

Is Max showing progress in his IEP?
- How do you know?
- What additional information do you wish was included? (For example, does Max have appropriate expressive language skills?) How would you obtain the needed information? How would that data help inform the IEP team and instructional plan?

Why did the SLP and teacher recommend push-in services during reading and writing instructional time?
- What supports could the SLP provide to improve literacy instruction for all students?
- Based on their training, what expertise do SLPs have that teachers do not? How do their skills complement each other?

What strategies and suggestions could the SLP provide the teacher? Specifically,
- How might the teacher explicitly prompt Max for correct sound production?
- What words or nonverbal gestures could the teacher use to cue him?
- When Max is writing, should the teacher give him opportunity to correct his work, such as on a spelling test?

For communicating with parents,
- How do the SLP and teacher work together to share information?
- How are grades and progress shared to show the accommodations and potential modifications provided?

Have you experienced push-in or coteaching experiences with an SLP?
- Is this something you could do in your school?
- What are the barriers to creating these collaborative teaching experiences?
- How could you ensure you have common planning and preparation time?
- What supports would you need from administration?

CASE STUDY 2: SARAIAH

Saraiah (suh-RYE-uh) is an 8-year-old, 3rd-grade student attending her local elementary school. She is eligible for special education and related services under "Other Health Impairment." When Saraiah was born, she was diagnosed as having spina bifida. Spina bifida occurs when part of the neural tube along the spine does not develop or close properly, leading to defects in the spinal cord and bones of the spine. For Saraiah, this means she is paralyzed from the waist down. As a result of the spina bifida, she requires two things from her local district to attend school: (1) specialized transportation to help her get to and from school daily and (2) an aide who assists her with clean intermittent catheterization as a way of relieving her bladder.

Saraiah can attend school and participate fully as a direct result of the related services she receives. Without the specialized transportation, she would not have a way to get to and from school. Without the aide who assists with the clean intermittent catheterization, she would not be able to come to school because she still requires assistance using the bathroom. Though we expect her to be able to do the clean intermittent catheterization herself within the next few years, right now it is necessary for her to have an aide to assist with this.

Saraiah is doing fine behaviorally and socially. She is an active member of her school community and has a lot of friends. Academically, the most recent evaluation information shows Saraiah is on level for reading, writing, and mathematics skills, but there are concerns in her executive functioning and organizational skills, which are negatively affecting her educational performance on grade-level academic tasks. In the classroom, Saraiah is almost always able to do all work asked of her correctly but relies on prompting for completion. Saraiah needs prompting to start assignments and complete assignments in all subject areas. There are routines set up for Saraiah to move to the small group table for independent work. When moved, Saraiah continues to need prompting to look back over her work to be sure she has completed all parts.

In math, Saraiah can compute equations accurately; however, when asked to complete multistep problems or word problems, she needs assistance to answer what is asked of her. Saraiah is making progress in learning how to organize her math thinking using bar modeling, part-part-whole, and place-value templates. Saraiah demonstrates similar issues with organizing her thinking in writing, which is especially noticeable, as the grade-level standards include prewriting (brainstorming), writing for a specific audience and purpose, and constructing a multiple-paragraph text with organized supporting details.

Questions to Consider

What are the related services Saraiah is receiving?
- Who is responsible for each?
- How and when are they documented?

Is the team using a consistent organizational format (e.g., daily planner, checklist) with Saraiah across settings?
- How are these used in academic tasks? Medical tasks?
- How could these support Saraiah's independence in skill development?
- Are copies provided for home use?
- What is the communication system among all team members?

How is Saraiah included as an active member of the team and self-advocate? Is Saraiah showing progress in her IEP?
- How do you know?
- What additional information do you wish was included? How would you obtain the needed information? How would that data help inform the IEP team and instructional plan?

CASE STUDY 3: ANGELUS

Angelus is a 15-year-old student with a medical diagnosis of autism who meets eligibility for special education services and related services under the category of "Autism Spectrum Disorder." The IEP team determined he needs academic, behavioral, and communication services in order to provide an appropriate education. Angelus's local school district does not have the services necessary to support him, so the IEP team determined 2 years ago that he should enroll in a nearby private school for students with autism. All the students in the private school require a high level of academic and behavioral support. The school has 41 students, ages 13 to 21. The current IEP team consists of his parents, representatives from his local school, the classroom teacher from the private school, and the related-service providers. While not all related-service personnel were able to attend the meeting, all provided written input to be considered in the meeting.

Angelus requires speech-language services due to his minimal communication skills and limited vocabulary. When requesting items he wants or needs, he uses simple one- and two-word phrases. For example, to ask for any type of treat or dessert, he requests cake. Angelus also often mimics phrases he has heard from the television show *Family Guy*. While these phrases can be humorous to those familiar with the show, they may negatively affect his ability to socialize with peers and understand appropriate language in a future job setting. The SLP and family have been implementing a low-tech augmentative/alternative communication (AAC) system of picture exchange to increase the length and complexity of communication options. As a result of his ongoing communication needs, Angelus receives speech-language therapy from an SLP three times a week for 30 minutes each time.

Angelus also requires occupational therapy to address daily challenges outside the scope of academic instruction. Angelus struggles with tactile sensitivities. His family is hoping he can learn to wear novel clothing items. Currently, he insists on wearing the same hat on the bus every day and only has three shirts he will wear. The occupational therapist (OT) is currently working with Angelus and his family on a program to support tolerating novel textures. As a result of his tactile sensitivities, he meets with an occupational therapist once a week for 30 minutes.

Angelus demonstrates some rather significant destructive behaviors. These include eloping due to loud noises, property destruction of new items that he does not want to touch due to tactile sensitivity, and noncompliance when he does not want to follow a given demand. The school has a dedicated board-certified behavior analyst (BCBA) who works with Angelus on behavioral goals. He has three behavioral goals in his IEP. The BCBA is in his classroom regularly.

Given the nature and extent of his individualized needs, Angelus's IEP includes a significant amount of information in the present level about his academic, behavioral, functional, and communication needs. The goals include academics, behavior, communication, and occupational therapy. While the related-service providers are primarily responsible for the quality and content of the goals, the classroom teacher is integrally involved in the instruction and intervention, as well as progress monitoring. The SLP, OT, and

BCBA provide direct services to Angelus, as well as consultative supports for the teacher. The classroom teacher works to generalize the targeted skills into the classroom and school settings and provides Angelus with opportunities for continued practice throughout the day. This level of collaborative work requires frequent communication among all the professionals involved in supporting Angelus. The teacher coordinates the schedule of services, progress monitoring, and communication among the various related-service providers, as well as provides Angelus's parents with a daily communication log with updates and ideas for continuity across both the home and school settings. Additionally, because Angelus receives his educational services at a school that is different from his local school, the private school teacher communicates with the special education case manager within the home school.

Questions to Consider

Is Angelus showing progress in his IEP?
- How do you know?
- What additional information do you wish was included in the case study? How would you obtain the needed information? How would that data help inform the IEP team and instructional plan?

How could the model of related services better support the student and teacher?

What is the process or format used to communicate progress on goals across settings?
- How do the related-service providers share feedback with the teacher?
- How does the team communicate about generalization of skills?
- How are strategies and tools communicated with home?
- Do families have a way to communicate what they are trying at home?

How often do the related-service providers observe the teacher work with Angelus?

Who is involved in deciding the communication purposes for the AAC trial?

What information is provided about Angelus's postsecondary goals and transition planning? What additional information is needed? What additional related-service providers or community agencies may need to be involved?

Appendix B

Supreme Court Cases Involving Related Services

IRVING INDEPENDENT SCHOOL DISTRICT V. TATRO
468 US 883 (1984)

The *Tatro* case involved Amber Tatro, an 8-year-old girl born with spina bifida. As a result, she had orthopedic and speech impairments and a neurogenic bladder, which prevented her from emptying her bladder voluntarily. Consequently, she needed to be catheterized every three or four hours to avoid injury to her kidneys. In accordance with accepted medical practice, clean intermittent catheterization (CIC), a procedure involving the insertion of a catheter into the urethra to drain the bladder, had been prescribed. The procedure is a simple one that may be performed in a few minutes by a layperson with less than an hour's training. Amber's parents, babysitter, and teenage brother were all qualified to administer CIC, and Amber was soon able to perform this procedure herself.

Originally, the district agreed to provide special education for Amber, who was then 3½ years old. In consultation with her parents, an IEP was developed for Amber and provided that Amber would attend early childhood development classes and receive special services, such as physical and occupational therapy. That program, however, made no provision for school personnel to administer CIC.

Amber's parents sought an injunction ordering the district to provide Amber with CIC and sought damages and attorney's fees. First, the parents invoked the Education of the Handicapped Act.[1] Because Texas received funding under that statute, the district was required to provide Amber with a "free appropriate public education," which is defined to include "related

---

1. The name was changed in 1990 to the Individuals with Disabilities Education Act (IDEA).

services." The parents argued that CIC is one such related service and invoked Section 504 of the Rehabilitation Act of 1973, which forbids an individual, by reason of a handicap, to be "excluded from the participation in, be denied the benefits of, or be subjected to discrimination under" any program receiving federal aid.

A *free appropriate public education* is explicitly defined as "special education and related services." The term *special education* means

- "specially designed instruction, at no cost to parents or guardians, to meet the unique needs of a handicapped child, including classroom instruction, instruction in physical education, home instruction, and instruction in hospitals and institutions."
- *Related services* are defined as

  transportation, and such developmental, corrective, and other supportive services (including speech pathology and audiology, psychological services, physical and occupational therapy, recreation, and medical and counseling services, except that such medical services shall be for diagnostic and evaluation purposes only) as may be required to assist a handicapped child to benefit from special education and includes the early identification and assessment of handicapping conditions in children.

The issue in this case is whether CIC was a related service the district was obliged to provide to Amber. The Supreme Court had two questions to address: First, whether CIC is a "supportive servic[e] . . . required to assist a handicapped child to benefit from special education,"[2] and second, whether CIC is excluded from this definition as a medical service serving purposes other than diagnosis or evaluation.

The Supreme Court ruled that CIC is a "supportive servic[e] . . . required to assist a handicapped child to benefit from special education." It is clear on this record that, without having CIC services available during the school day, Amber cannot attend school and thereby "benefit from special education." CIC services therefore fall squarely within the definition of a *supportive service*.

The court noted, "Congress sought primarily to make public education available to handicapped children" and "to make such access meaningful." A service that enables a handicapped child to remain at school during the day is an important means of providing the child with the meaningful access to education that Congress envisioned. The act makes specific provision for services, like transportation, for example, that do no more than enable a child

---

2. The term handicap was a part of the law when the cases in Appendix B were heard. The accepted term now is student with a disability.

to be physically present in class; and the act specifically authorizes grants for schools to alter buildings and equipment to make them accessible to the handicapped.

The court held that CIC services in this case qualify as a "supportive servic[e] . . . required to assist a handicapped child to benefit from special education."

The Court also held that provision of CIC is not a "medical servic[e]," which a school is required to provide only for purposes of diagnosis or evaluation. The regulations define *related services* for handicapped children to include "school health services," which are defined in turn as "services provided by a qualified school nurse or other qualified person." *Medical services* are defined as "services provided by a licensed physician." Thus, the secretary determined that the services of a school nurse otherwise qualifying as a "related service" are not subject to exclusion as a "medical service" but that the services of a physician are excludable as such.

This definition of *medical services* is a reasonable interpretation of congressional intent. Although Congress devoted little discussion to the medical-services exclusion, the secretary could reasonably have concluded that it was designed to spare schools from an obligation to provide a service that might well prove unduly expensive and beyond the range of their competence. From this understanding of congressional purpose, the secretary could reasonably have concluded that Congress intended to impose the obligation to provide school nursing services.

Congress plainly required schools to hire various specially trained personnel to help handicapped children, such as "trained occupational therapists, speech therapists, psychologists, social workers and other appropriately trained personnel." School nurses have long been a part of the educational system, and the secretary could therefore reasonably conclude that school nursing services are not the sort of burden that Congress intended to exclude as a medical service. By limiting the medical-services exclusion to the services of a physician or hospital, both far more expensive, the secretary has given a permissible construction to the provision.

The district argued that CIC was a medical service, even though it may be provided by a nurse or trained layperson. Nurses in the district are authorized to dispense oral medications and administer emergency injections in accordance with a physician's prescription. This kind of service for nonhandicapped children is difficult to distinguish from the provision of CIC to the handicapped. The court stated it would be strange indeed if Congress, in attempting to extend special services to handicapped children, were unwilling to guarantee them services of a kind that are routinely provided to the nonhandicapped.

To keep in perspective the obligation to provide services that relate to both the health and educational needs of handicapped students, the court noted several limitations that should minimize the burden the petitioner (district) fears. First, to be entitled to related services, a child must be handicapped so as to require special education. In the absence of a handicap that requires special education, the need for what otherwise might qualify as a related service does not create an obligation under the act.

Second, only those services necessary to aid a handicapped child to benefit from special education must be provided, regardless of how easily a school nurse or layperson could furnish them. For example, if a particular medication or treatment may appropriately be administered to a handicapped child other than during the school day, a school is not required to provide nursing services to administer it.

Third, the regulations state that school nursing services must be provided only if they can be performed by a nurse or other qualified person, not if they must be performed by a physician. It bears mentioning here that not even the services of a nurse are required; as is conceded, a layperson with minimal training is qualified to provide CIC.

Finally, the court noted that the parents are not asking the district to provide equipment that Amber needs for CIC. They seek only the services of a qualified person at the school. The court concluded that the provision of CIC to Amber is not subject to exclusion as a medical service and affirmed that CIC is a related service under the Education of the Handicapped Act.

Questions to Consider

1. What question was decided in this case? What was the decision?
2. What is the difference between medical services and supportive services in terms of special education?
3. When must a school provide a related service?
4. Are districts obligated to provide related services to students who do not receive special education?
5. What are the limitations on related services?
6. When considering students with medical needs, has your perspective on related services changed after reading about this case? If so, how?
7. "A service that enables a handicapped child to remain at school during the day is an important means of providing the child with the meaningful access to education."
   - How does this further your understanding of how related services support accessibility?
   - How does this reinforce your understanding of free appropriate public education (FAPE)?

CEDAR RAPIDS COMMUNITY SCHOOL DISTRICT V. GARRET F. (96-1793) 526 US 66 (1999)

The *Garret F.* case involved a student in the Cedar Rapids Community School District in the state of Iowa. Garret F. was described as a friendly, creative, and intelligent young man. When Garret was 4 years old, his spinal column was severed in a motorcycle accident. Though paralyzed from the neck down, his mental capacities were unaffected. He was able to speak, to control his motorized wheelchair through the use of a puff-and-suck straw, and to operate a computer with a device that responds to head movements. He attended general education classes, with great academic success. Garret was, however, ventilator dependent and therefore required a responsible individual nearby to attend to certain physical needs while he was in school.

During Garret's early years at school, his family provided for his physical care during the school day. When he was in kindergarten, his 18-year-old aunt volunteered as his attendant; in the next 4 years, his family used settlement proceeds they received after the accident, their insurance, and other resources to employ a licensed practical nurse. After that, Garret's mother requested the district to accept financial responsibility for the health care services that Garret required during the school day. The district denied the request, believing it was not legally obligated to provide continuous one-on-one nursing services.

Relying on both IDEA and Iowa law, Garret's mother requested a hearing and presented extensive evidence concerning Garret's special needs, the district's treatment of other students with disabilities, and the assistance provided to other ventilator-dependent children in other parts of the country. The initial hearing found the district had about 17,500 students, of whom approximately 2,200 needed some form of special education or special services. Although Garret was the only ventilator-dependent student in the district, most of the health care services that he needed were already provided for some other students; the "primary difference between Garret's situation and that of other students is his dependency on his ventilator for life support." The administrative law judge (ALJ) noted the parties disagreed over the training or licensure required for the care and supervision of such students and that those providing such care in other parts of the country ranged from nonlicensed personnel to registered nurses. However, the district did not contend that only a licensed physician could provide the services in question.

The ALJ explained that federal law requires children with a variety of health impairments be provided with "special education and related services" when their disabilities adversely affect their academic performance and that such children should be educated to the maximum extent appropriate with children who are not disabled. In addition, the ALJ explained that applicable federal regulations distinguish between "school health services," which are provided by a "qualified school nurse or other qualified person," and "medical services," which are provided by a licensed physician. The district must provide the former but need not provide the latter [except, of course, those "medical services" that are for diagnostic or evaluation purposes, §1401(a)(17)]. According to the ALJ, the distinction in the regulations does not just depend on the "title of the person providing the service"; instead, the medical-services exclusion is limited to services that are "in the special training, knowledge, and judgment of a physician to carry out." The ALJ thus concluded that IDEA required the district to bear financial responsibility for all of the services in dispute, including continuous nursing services.

In the Supreme Court, the school board did not argue that Garret's care constituted medical services. Instead, it proposed several other factors should be considered, including "whether the care is continuous or intermittent" and the expense of the service. The Supreme Court decision noted that the school district's proposed test was not supported by the statute's text or any other regulation. Focusing on the issue of expense, the court rejected accepting a cost-based standard, arguing that doing so would have required it to engage in judicial lawmaking without any congressional guidance. In the court's view, Congress intended IDEA to "open the door of public education" to all qualified students and to require school boards to "educate handicapped children with non-handicapped children whenever possible."

Relying on the precedent from the *Tatro* case, the court ruled that a school must fund such related services to help guarantee that students like Garret had an opportunity to attend school.

Questions to Consider

1. What question was decided in this case? What was the decision?
2. When must a school provide a related service?
3. What is the difference, if any, between the decision in this case and the *Tatro* decision?
4. What are the limitations on related services?
5. What is the controversy regarding complex health services as related services under IDEA?
6. Why is it important that a "cost-based standard" was rejected?
7. What is the bright-line test for determining whether a school needs to provide a related service?
8. In this case, Garret was the only ventilator-dependent student in his district. What does this tell you about the importance of related services?
9. How does this case reinforce your understanding of free appropriate public education?

Key Terms

activities of daily living (ADLs): activities related to personal care, which can include bathing or showering, dressing, eating, walking, and toileting.

aide: a person assigned to assist or support. In special education, an aide can be listed as a service or support on the IEP, with the person assigned to assist or support a student with disabilities with a particular task or function for the student to access special education services. Examples include a health care aide, transportation aide, and so on. Other terms include *paraprofessional, parapro, classroom attendant*.

assistive technology (AT): a device or service used by individuals with disabilities to assist with functions that might be difficult. Walkers, wheelchairs, screen readers, picture-exchange communication systems, and magnifying devices are all considered assistive technology.

audiologists: specially trained professionals who help prevent, diagnose, and treat hearing and balance disorders for people of all ages.

autism: a developmental disability significantly affecting verbal and nonverbal communication and social interaction, usually evident before age 3 and adversely affecting a child's educational performance.

better practices: practices that may go beyond what the law actually requires but enable special educators to meet the legal requirements of developing and implementing special education programs so students make progress in light of their unique educational needs.

bright-line test: a clearly stated and easy-to-follow rule.

chronic health conditions: health conditions that last 1 year or more, require ongoing medical attention, and/or limit activities of daily living.

collaboration: two or more people working together to achieve a goal or accomplish a task.

consultation: related-service providers provide training to educators who work directly with a student.

coteaching: a collaborative approach to instruction in which two professionals work together to plan and implement instruction, usually for a class that includes students with special education services.

extended school year (ESY): individualized services to help a child maintain skills and not lose progress made toward goals during an extended period when school is not in session, such as summer break.

free appropriate public education (FAPE): the education to which every student is entitled under IDEA. Every student is entitled to an education that is appropriate for their unique needs and that is provided at no cost to the parents or guardians.

harness: a form of protective equipment designed to safeguard a person during transit, such as on a school bus. The harness fits around a person's legs, over their arms, and around their torso.

IEP team: a team of people who develops the individualized education program (IEP). IDEA requires certain team members, including a parent or guardian, a general education teacher, a special education teacher, a school district representative, and an expert who can interpret the evaluation results. Others, such as related-service providers, should be invited based on the student's individualized needs.

individualized education program (IEP): a legal document between the school district and the parents that defines special education services for an individual child eligible to receive special education; also individualized education *plan*.

Individuals with Disabilities Education Act (IDEA): a law that guarantees educational rights to all students with disabilities and makes it illegal for school districts to refuse to educate a student based on their disability.

least restrictive environment (LRE): a mandate in IDEA that students with disabilities should be educated to the maximum extent appropriate with their nondisabled peers.

medical services: services that can only be provided by a licensed physician; exempt from the definition of *related services*, unless needed for diagnostic or evaluative purposes.

occupational therapy (OT): services to improve, develop, or restore functions of activities required for daily life.

orientation and mobility (O&M): a profession focused on instructing individuals with visual impairments or blindness on safe and effective travel throughout their environments.

physical therapy (PT): service to address posture, muscular strength, mobility, and organization of movements.

present levels of academic achievement and functional performance (PLAAFP): a component of an individualized education program (IEP) that defines a student's strengths and weaknesses, current levels of academic achievement, and functional performance. The information in the PLAAFP directs the creation of goals and determination of needed special education and related services. Sometimes referred to as *present levels*, *PLEP*, *PLAP*, *PLOP*, and other abbreviated terms used locally in districts and regions.

progress monitoring: scheduled data collection to monitor a student's progress toward a goal.

recreational therapy (RT): a systematic process that uses recreation and other activity-based interventions to address the assessed needs of individuals with illnesses or disabling conditions to improve psychological and physical health, recovery, and well-being.

regulations: instructions written by the executive branch that provide direction on how to implement and enforce laws passed by Congress. Special educators must be aware of federal and state regulations pertaining to special education law.

related services: transportation and such developmental, corrective, and other supportive services required to help a child with a disability benefit from special education.

response to intervention (RtI): A multitiered approach to the early identification and support of students with learning and behavior needs.

special education: education specially designed to meet the unique needs of a child with a disability.

speech-language services: services to address deficits in (1) the mechanical aspects of speaking (voice, fluency, articulation); (2) the language-based skills of understanding and expressing thoughts and ideas (receptive and expressive language), reading, writing, processing information, and interacting socially; and (3) feeding and swallowing skill deficits that interfere with safety, well-being, and educational performance.

value-add: something or someone who adds value and benefits the team, project, or purpose.

References

American Academy of Pediatrics (AAP). (2023). www.aap.org
American Occupational Therapy Association (AOTA). (2022). *Evidence-based practice and knowledge translation.* https://www.aota.org/practice/practice-essentials/evidencebased-practiceknowledge-translation
American Occupational Therapy Association (AOTA). (2023). https://www.aota.org
American Physical Therapy Association (APTA). (2022a). https://www.apta.org
American Physical Therapy Association (APTA). (2022b). *Patient care.* https://www.apta.org/patient-care
American School Counselor Association (ASCA). (2022). https://www.schoolcounselor.org
American Speech-Language-Hearing Association (ASHA). (2002). *Guidelines for audiology service provision in and for schools.* https://www.asha.org/policy/gl2002-00005/
American Speech-Language-Hearing Association (ASHA). (2015). *School-based speech-language pathologists: Who we are and what we do* [PowerPoint slides]. https://www.asha.org/siteassets/uploadedFiles/What-SLPs-Do.pdf
American Speech-Language-Hearing Association (ASHA). (2022). *Certification.* https://www.asha.org/certification/
Bateman, D. F., & Cline, J. L. (2016). *A teacher's guide to special education.* ASCD.
American Speech-Language-Hearing Association (ASHA). (2019). *Special education law case studies: A review from practitioners.* Rowman & Littlefield.
Center for Parent Information and Resources. (2020, June). *Disability and special education acronyms.* https://www.parentcenterhub.org/acronyms/
Cedar Rapids Community School District v. Garret F., a minor by his mother and next friend, Charlene P., 526 US 66 (1999).
Goran, L., Harkins Monaco, E. A., Yell, M. L., Shriner, J., & Bateman, D. (2020). Pursuing academic and functional advancement: Goals, services, and measuring progress. *Teaching Exceptional Children*, 52(5), 333–343.
Individuals with Disabilities Education Act (IDEA), 20 USC § 1400 et seq. (2006).

Individuals with Disabilities Education Act (IDEA) Regulations, 34 CFR § 300 et seq. (2006).

IRIS Center. (2023a). *IEPs: Developing high-quality individualized education programs.* https://iris.peabody.vanderbilt.edu/module/iep01/

IRIS Center. (2023b). *IEPs: How administrators can support the development and implementation of high-quality IEPs.* https://iris.peabody.vanderbilt.edu/module/iep02/

Irving Independent School District v. Tatro, 468 US 883 (1984).

Markelz, A. M., & Bateman, D. F. (2021). *The essentials of special education law.* Rowman & Littlefield.

Morin, A. (2014). *Extended school year services: What you need to know.* Understood.org. https://www.understood.org/en/articles/extended-school-year-services-what-you-need-to-know

Murawski, W. W., & Scott, K. L. (eds.). (2017). *What really works with exceptional learners.* Corwin Press.

National Association of School Nurses (NASN). (2023). www.nasn.org

National Association of School Psychologists (NASP). (2021). *Who are school psychologists.* https://www.nasponline.org/about-school-psychology/who-are-school-psychologists

National Council for Therapeutic Recreation Certification (NCTRC). (2023). *About recreational therapy.* https://www.nctrc.org/about-nctrc/about-recreational-therapy/

National Council on Interpreting in Health Care (NCIHC). (n.d.). www.ncihc.org

National Federation for the Blind (NFB). (2023). https://nfb.org

National Institute on Deafness and Other Communication Disorders (NIDCD). (2017). *Mission.* https://www.nih.gov/about-nih/what-we-do/nih-almanac/national-institute-deafness-other-communication-disorders-nidcd

Public Broadcasting System. (2002). *Misunderstood minds.* https://www.pbs.org/wgbh/misunderstoodminds/

Rehabilitation Act of 1973, Section 504, 29 USC § 701 et seq.

School Social Work Association of America (SSWAA). (n.d.). https://www.sswaa.org

Understood.org. (n.d.). https://www.understood.org/

US Department of Education. (2021). *IDEA annual report to Congress—Office of special education programs.*

Yell, M. L. (2019). *The law and special education* (5th ed.). Pearson.

Yell, M. L., Bateman, D. F., & Shriner, J. G. (2021). *Developing educationally meaningful and legally sound IEPs.* Rowman & Littlefield.

Index

Note: Page numbers in *italics* refer to tables.

abbreviations, 118
ABCD-T method, 30
absences from school, 84
accommodations, 90
accountability, 26
acronyms, 118
administrators, 26, 104–5, 123–24
allocation of staff and resources, 26
American Occupational Therapy Association (AOTA), 101
American Speech-Language Hearing Association (ASHA), 101
Angelus (case study), 132–34
annual performance goals, 25
AOTA (American Occupational Therapy Association), 101
articulation skills, 99
art therapy, 9
ASHA (American Speech-Language Hearing Association), 101
assessments. *See* evaluations; health assessment; progress monitoring; transportation assessment
assistive technology, 10

audiology services, 10–11, 119–20. *See also* hearing loss
Autism Spectrum Disorder case study, 132–34

Bateman, David F., 116
BCBA (board-certified behavior analyst), 133–34
behavior of students: in case study, 133–34; requiring aides, 63; transportation and, 57–58, 60, 61–62, 63, 66–67. *See also* counseling services; psychological services
board-certified behavior analyst (BCBA), 133–34
breath-control exercises, 99
bright-line test, 15, 47–48. *See also* school health and school nurse services

case studies: Angelus, 132–34; Max, 129–31; Saraiah, 131–32
Cedar Rapids Community School District v. Garret F., 15, 23, 139–40

CIC (clean intermittent catheterization), 131–32, 135–38
classroom teachers. *See* general education teachers and classrooms
clean intermittent catheterization (CIC), 131–32, 135–38
Cline, Jenifer, 116
cochlear implants, 7–9, 119. *See also* audiology services
collaboration, 97–98, 100–101, 106–7
communication: IEP document as tool for, 25; importance of, 102–3; national organizations providing guidance on, 117; with related-services professionals, 102–7; students requiring assistance with, 64
compliance-monitoring process, 27
confidentiality, 37, 53–54, 82
cost of related services, 7, 23, 125
counseling services, 11, 13, 120, 121. *See also* psychological services
COVID-19 pandemic, 16

Day in the Life summaries: of Baleigh, 108, *108–10,* 111; of Mallory, 111, *111–13,* 113
deaf-blind children, 12
demographics in IEP, 28
Developing Educationally Meaningful and Legally Sound IEPs (Yell, Bateman, and Shriner), 116
devices/equipment, 7–9, 59, 64–66, 85, 131–32, 135–38
diet restrictions, 85–86, *87*
districts, 36, 83
do-not-resuscitate orders, 67

early identification/assessment of disabilities, 11, 120
early literacy skills, 99
Education of the Handicapped Act, 135–38. *See also* Individuals with Disabilities Education Act (IDEA)
eligibility for related services, 4, 6–7, 124–25

emergency exits, 63
emergency procedures, 85
equipment/devices, 7–9, 59, 64–66, 85, 131–32, 135–38
The Essentials of Special Education Law (Markelz and Bateman), 116
ESY (extended school year), 31
evaluations: for eligibility, 4, 6–7, 124–25; for identifying disabilities, 11; interpreters for, 34; state and district assessments, 36; of student progress, 26
exclusions, 7–9, 48, 119, 125, 136–38, 140
expertise of related-service providers, 101–2, 107
extended school year (ESY), 31
external service providers, 103

FAPE (free appropriate public education), 1, 7, 23–24, 125, 135–38
federal laws. *See* Education of the Handicapped Act; Individuals with Disabilities Education Act (IDEA)
feeding/diet issues, 85–86, *87,* 90
fine-motor activities, 86
formal collaboration, 100
free appropriate public education (FAPE), 1, 7, 23–24, 125, 135–38

Garret F. Supreme Court decision, 15, 23, 139–40
general education teachers and classrooms: advice for, 123; important IEP points for, 36–37; location for related services and, 31, 32, 36, 59–60; roles of, 33, 34, 37, 133–34; supports for, 30–31; training related-service providers, 102
goals/objectives, 35, 36, 61, 126

health assessment: about, 81; confidentiality and, 82; introductory information, 82–84, 93–94; key terms, 91, 93; next steps section,

88, 95; nonannotated copy, 93–96; questions to consider, 93; school day needs, *87,* 89, 92, 96; specific training needs, 86, 88, 95. *See also* school health and school nurse services

hearing loss, 7–9, 10, 12, 119. *See also* audiology services

IDEA. *See* Individuals with Disabilities Education Act (IDEA)

IEPs (individualized education plans): changing, 6, 27, 32–33, 37; components of, 27–33; developing, 105, 118; IDEA requirements, 3–7, 22–23; purposes of, 21–22, 25–27; as road map, 25; tips for, 22–25. *See also* IEP team members

IEP team members: advice for, 126; communicating with, 103; progress monitoring, 6–7; reevaluating IEPS, 32–33; related-service decisions and, 2–3, 5–9, 17, 23, 53–54; related-service providers as, 6–7, 24, 35, 105–6, 126; roles, 33–35; signature requirements, 28. *See also* IEPs (individualized education plans)

independence, areas of, 90, 91

Individuals with Disabilities Education Act (IDEA): defining related services, 9–17; exclusions, 7–9; IEP requirements, 3–7, 22–23; law and regulations, 118–22. *See also* Education of the Handicapped Act; *specific related services*

informal collaboration, 100–101

interpreting services, 12, 120

interprofessional collaborative practice (IPCP), 101

IRIS website, 118

Irving Independent School District v. Tatro, 15, 23, 135–38

key terms, 141–43; for health assessment, 91, 93; for providers, 114; for related services, 18–19; for requirements, 38–39; for resources, 127; for transportation assessment, 71–72

language skills, 99

LEA (Local Education Agency) representatives, 34

least restrictive environment (LRE), 32, 36

Local Education Agency (LEA) representatives, 34

location for related services, 31, 32, 36, 59–60

LRE (least restrictive environment), 32, 36

lunch period, 85–86, *87,* 90

management, 26

Markelz, Andrew M., 116

Max (case study), 129–31

medical and health services: advice about, 124, 125–26; devices/ equipment, 7–9, 59, 64–66, 85, 131–32, 135–38; medication, 59, 85; national organizations for, 117; recommendations from physicians, 23; regulations, 120; school health and school nurse services comparison, 140; transportation and, 57, 66–67. *See also* health assessment; school health and school nurse services

Misunderstood Minds website, 118

mobility and orientation assistance, 12–13, 86, 88, 102, 120–21

Murawski, Wendy, 116

National Association of School Psychologists (NASP), 101

notice of procedural safeguards, 28

nurses. *See* health assessment; medical and health services; school health and school nurse services

occupational therapy (OT), 12, 120, 133–34
orientation and mobility services (O&M), 12–13, 86, 88, 102, 120–21

paraprofessionals, 17
parents/guardians: counseling and training, 13, 121; progress updates provided to, 103; role of, 34; transportation notifications to, 70–71
peer socialization, 91
peer transportation, 56
percentages, 126
performance of students. *See* goals/objectives; Present Levels of Academic Achievement and Functional Performance (PLAAFP); progress monitoring
physical services, 117, 121
physical therapy, 13
placement for related services, 31, 32, 36, 59–60
PLEP. *See* Present Levels of Academic Achievement and Functional Performance (PLAAFP)
Present Levels of Academic Achievement and Functional Performance (PLAAFP), 29, 35–36, 61, 101
principals, 26, 104–5, 123–24
procedural notices, 28
procedural safeguards, 35
progress monitoring, 6–7, 30, 103
psychological services, 13–14, 34, 101, 125–26. *See also* counseling services

recreation, 14, 121
regulations. *See* Individuals with Disabilities Education Act (IDEA)
rehabilitation counseling, 14–15, 121–22

related-service providers: as collaborators, 97–98, 100–101, 106–7; communicating with, 102–7; for direct services, 98–100; expertise of, 101–2, 107; health assessment and, 83; on IEP team, 6–7, 24, 35, 105–6, 126; key terms, 114; needs of student *vs.* staff availability, 24–25; questions to consider, 114; summary, 113. *See also* Day in the Life summaries
related services: changes to, 32, 56, 126; costs, 7, 23, 125; defined, 1–2, 9–17, 22–23, 119, 136; exclusions, 7–9, 48, 119, 125, 136–38, 140; key terms, 18–19, 38–39; location for, 31, 32, 36, 59–60; questions to consider, 19, 39; regulations for, 118–22; sample list of, 2, 4–5; summary, 17–18; timing of, 24, 36, 126. *See also* IEPs (individualized education plans); related-service providers; resources for related services; specific related services
resources for related services: advice about, 123–26; books, 116; key terms, 127; national organizations, 117; online, 118; questions to consider, 127–28; regulations, 118–22

safety, 57, 63
Saraiah (case study), 131–32
scheduling of related services, 126
school attendance, 84
school bus transportation. *See* transportation assessment; transportation regulations
school day needs assessment, 87
school health and school nurse services: CIC, 131–32, 135–38; defined, 15; expertise of providers, 102; medical services *vs.*, 140; regulations, 122. *See also* health assessment; medical and health services
Scott, Kathy Lynn, 116

self-care, 84, 85, 88, 90
sensory needs of students, 58
Shriner, James G., 116
small-group therapy, 99
social, emotional, and psychological services, 117. *See also* behavior of students; counseling services; psychological services
social acceptance. *See* peer socialization
social work services in school, 15–16, 122
special considerations section of IEP, 28–29
special education: defined, 136; related services provided only with, 4–5, 22–23; teacher roles, 34; tips for classroom teachers, 36–37
Special Education Law Case Studies (Bateman, Cline, and Steele), 116
specific related services: about, 9; art therapy, 9; assistive technology, 10; audiology services, 10–11, 119–20; counseling services, 11, 13, 120, 121; early identification and assessment of disabilities, 11, 120; interpreting services, 12, 120; occupational therapy, 12, 120, 133–34; orientation and mobility services, 12–13, 86, 88, 102, 120–21; parent/guardian counseling and training, 13, 121; physical therapy, 13; psychological services, 13–14, 34, 101, 125–26; recreation, 14, 121; rehabilitation counseling, 14–15, 121–22; social work services in school, 15–16, 122. *See also* health assessment; medical and health services; school health and school nurse services; speech-language pathology; transportation assessment
speech-language pathology: Baleigh's Day in the Life summary, 108, *108–10*, 111; case studies, 129–31, 132–34; defined, 16; direct service providers, 99–100, 102, 111, 113;

Mallory's Day in the Life summary, 111, *111–13*, 113; regulations, 122
spina bifida, 131–32, 135–38
staff: allocation of, 26; availability *vs.* needs of student, 24–25; training of, 65, 67, 69–70, 85, 86, 88, 95. *See also* IEP team members; related-service providers
state assessments, 36
state regulations, 21
Steele, Jonathan D., 116
students: annual performance goals, 25; goals and objectives in IEP, 29–30; role in IEPs, 33–34
summer programs, 31
Supreme Court cases: *Cedar Rapids Community School District v. Garret F.,* 15, 23, 139–40; *Irving Independent School District v. Tatro,* 15, 23, 135–38
surgically implanted devices, 119

Tatro Supreme Court decision, 15, 23, 135–38
A Teacher's Guide to Special Education (Bateman and Cline), 116
technology services, 8
test rides on buses/vans, 67–68
toileting needs, 85, *87,* 88, 90
transportation assessment: about, 53–54; behavioral concerns, 57–58, 60, 61–62, 63, 66–67; changes in, 56, 57–58; equipment assistance, 64–66; general information, 54–56; key terms, 71–72; medical concerns, 57, 66–67; next steps required, 69–70; nonannotated copy, 72–80; other concerns noted in, 68–69; parent/guardian notifications, 70–71; pick-up and drop-off considerations, 59–60, 62; questions to consider, 72; seating on bus/van, 56, 60–61; supervision/assistance needs, 62–63; test rides, 67–68; weather factors, 58
transportation regulations, 16–17, 122

understood.org website, 118

ventilator-dependent students, 139–40
vision specialists, 100
vocational rehabilitation (VR) agencies, 15

weather factors in transportation assessment, 58
welcoming attitude, 104–5, 106
What Really Works with Exceptional Learners (Murawski and Scott), 116

Yell, Mitchell L., 116

About the Authors

Lisa Goran, PhD, CCC-SLP, is an associate teaching professor in the Department of Special Education at the University of Missouri, where she serves as the director of teacher education and director of undergraduate studies for special education. She teaches and coordinates courses in special education for students pursuing teacher certification. She is a speech-language pathologist who has worked in school, clinical, and private practice settings. As a special educator, she taught students with disabilities in self-contained and resource classrooms and cotaught in general education classrooms. She served as a building-level department chair for special education. Dr. Goran earned a PhD in special education from the University of Missouri. She is active in national- and state-level professional organizations related to speech-language pathology (ASHA, MSHA); special education (CEC, CASE, DLD, TED, MO-CASE); and teacher education (AACTE, MACTE). She recently coauthored chapters in *Developing Educationally Meaningful and Legally Compliant IEPs* and *Sexuality Education for Students with Disabilities* and an article for a special issue of *Teaching Exceptional Children* focusing on legally proficient IEPs.

David F. Bateman, PhD, is a principal researcher at the American Institutes for Research and a professor emeritus at Shippensburg University in the Department of Educational Leadership and Special Education, where he taught courses on special education law, assessment, and development of IEPs. He was a due-process hearing officer for Pennsylvania for more than 580 hearings. He uses his knowledge of litigation in special education to assist school districts in providing appropriate supports for students with disabilities and to prevent and recover from due-process hearings. He has been a classroom teacher of students with learning disabilities, behavior disorders, intellectual disability, and hearing impairments. Dr. Bateman earned a PhD in special education from the University of Kansas. He recently coauthored *A Principal's Guide to Special Education*; *A Teacher's Guide to Special Education*; *Special Education Leadership: Building Effective Programming in Schools*; *Developing Educationally Meaningful and Legally Sound IEPs*; and *Current Trends and Issues in Special Education*. He was coeditor of a special issue of *Teaching Exceptional Children* focusing on legally proficient IEPs.

Kristin C. Wikel (contributor, chapter 5) is the manager of the Riley Hospital for Children School Program. She has worked at Riley Hospital for Children since 2003. Her background is in education. She has a master's degree in special education, where she is licensed to work with students who are in kindergarten through 12th grade. She is a licensed special education director for students in preschool through 12th grade. Kristin is completing her dissertation at Ball State University for her PhD in special education with an emphasis on educational leadership. Kristin is extremely passionate about working with and advocating for students with chronic medical, physical, and mental health conditions.

www.ingramcontent.com/pod-product-compliance
Lightning Source LLC
Chambersburg PA
CBHW071821230426
43670CB00013B/2524